Reviews for
Discover The Entrepreneur Within

"The definitive book on business launch, in reality three books in one: the essence of entrepreneurship; the mechanics of a business; and, most importantly, how an entrepreneur can live a great life." – Robert J. Jordan, CEO, Association of Interim Executives, Author of *How They Did It: Billion Dollar Insights from the Heart of America.*

"It's said that some learn by doing, others by reading, but Professor Syal has done both to an uncommon degree... in this book he has synthesized a lifetime of experience into a highly readable book that I wish someone had given to me 40 years ago. Whether starting a business or starting in business, this is a book that will make you think about integrity, passion, discipline and teamwork, as well as the nuts and bolts that are essential and common to all successful companies." - James Steinback, Retired President and Owner, Magnecraft Electric Inc.

"*Discover The Entrepreneur Within* is the ideal guide for anyone serious about launching a business. It presents an engaging and practical work plan to solve a meaningful problem, understand customers, plan for economic sustainability, and lead a team for exceptional execution. Moreover, it offers wisdom to focus on living versus making a living. If every ambitious Millennial implements these concepts, the difference that they make will change the world. " – Laura McKee, CEO, Autistic Home Support Services.

"*Discover The Entrepreneur Within* is a great summary of Verinder's thinking that is worthwhile reading for teenagers and seniors. His concepts resonate with our students here at Northwestern as well as those from around the world. I know this firsthand since Verinder recently led our teaching team for a program where we hosted 25 entrepreneurs from 23 different African countries for the US State Department....They left after 6 weeks truly transformed and a great source of pride for Verinder and our entire Center since they will be future entrepreneurs and leaders in their countries." – Professor Mike Marasco, Director, Farley Center for Entrepreneurship and Innovation, Northwestern University.

"Verinder Syal's classes have long been among the most highly rated by Northwestern University students, and his new book clearly shows why. Its writing is fast paced and full of good humor, while working through the pragmatic consumer-focused details (of starting a business).... However, what really makes this book special within the field is the second half where Verinder works students through issues of leadership and ethics that go to the core of creating ventures.... I can see why students tell me that it's so life changing." Professor Mark Witte, Director, Undergraduate Studies in Economics, Northwestern University.

"Professor Syal has accomplished the very difficult task of (capturing) the essential ingredient for entrepreneurial success, and that is one's personal responsibility that arises from "within" for your aspirations, not only in business but in life....A wonderful narrative ... to the collective spirit of human achievement that begins with accepting the responsibility to lead oneself in an ethically, moral and sustainable way." – Dan Brown, Founder, Logger Head Tools, Professor of Design, Northwestern University.

"Must read for budding entrepreneurs and start ups! His deep understanding of businesses and entrepreneurship comes through in this book as he is able to address each and every question that crosses an entrepreneurs mind especially when at start up phase....You leave his class a better person with a clear vision for your business and life." – Muthoni Nduhiu, CEO, Mastermind Africa Alliance, Kenya.

"...is a must read book for potential and existing business owners... The book offers inspiration and information on idea generation, marketing, management, finance, business plan, technology, latest trends and strategies.... His passion and listening skills are relayed into succinct coaching thoughts that are both plausible and action oriented." - Felix Dela Klutse, Editor-In-Chief of *Business Day* Newspaper, Ghana.

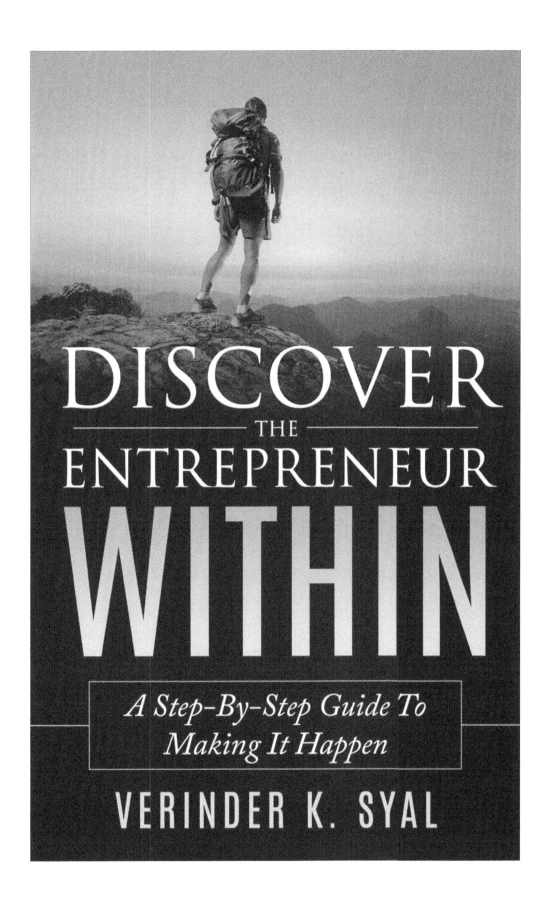

DISCOVER
— THE —
ENTREPRENEUR
WITHIN

A Step-By-Step Guide To Making It Happen

VERINDER K. SYAL

Illustrations: Adam Zalabany

Second Edition 2017

Published by Thoughtful Simplicity, Winnetka, IL
www.thoughtfulsimplicity.com

ISBN-13: 978-0692924648

ISBN-10: 0692924647

CONTENTS

FOREWORD

As someone who has been fortunate enough to serve in almost every possible role in startups and has devoted the past 10 years of my life to teaching and leading a center focused on entrepreneurship, I am always asked: *Can you teach entrepreneurship? Most people seem like they are born entrepreneurs.*

My answer is always the same: Entrepreneurs are not born. They are people who pursue their passions with discipline. They are leaders that understand what they are good and bad at and build teams to accentuate the positive and remove the negative. They are risk takers who understand the implications of the decisions they make. They are teachers who take great pride in fostering the development and growth of their team members.

All of us have passion; the entrepreneurs among us know how to focus that passion. All of us are entrepreneurs at our core. Very few of us understand how to tap that core. Verinder has done it and has dedicated his life to help others do the same. I am so glad that he chose to "bottle" his thinking into a book so all of you can learn what our Northwestern students have already figured out.

Teaching entrepreneurship is a great source of joy for me and all my colleagues. Verinder Syal is a colleague who not only is a phenomenal teacher but also a truly special person.

Teaching is a passion and a great teacher changes people lives. Verinder Syal is a great teacher who also has the discipline to document his thoughts in this book. *Discover The Entrepreneur Within* is a great summary of Verinder's thinking that is worthwhile reading for teenagers and seniors. His concepts resonate with our students here at Northwestern as well as those from around the world. I know this firsthand since Verinder recently led our teaching team for a program where we hosted 25 entrepreneurs from 23 different African countries for the US State Department-Mandela Washington Fellowship for Young African Leaders. Some of these students came from very early stage economies, but it did not matter. They left after 6 weeks truly transformed and a great source of pride for Verinder and our entire Center since they will be future entrepreneurs and leaders in their countries.

What is Verinder's magic formula? It is very simple common sense thinking that many of us forget about given the challenges of every day life. Verinder reminds us that great ideas only become great if they have a great team and address a real problem or need. He sorts through all of the frameworks and jargon to provide the reader with a simple set of rules and advice to succeed as an entrepreneur.

Verinder's approach works. I see it firsthand. His former students are so passionate about his impact on their lives that they stay in touch and even organize unofficial last lectures talks for him. I worry that Verinder does not sleep enough since he is always making time for a call, coffee, breakfast or lunch with current and former students. Verinder's home has become a form of a retreat and counseling center for current and former students. Words cannot express my thanks to Verinder's wife, Leia and their dog Biggins, for allowing him to devote significant time to his students, teaching and writing.

This book can truly help you start a new chapter in your life, but that can only happen if you have the desire and discipline to do so. Discover the entrepreneur within you so that you can truly live life at a higher level.

Michael A Marasco
Clinical Professor
Director, Farley Center for Entrepreneurship and Innovation
McCormick School of Engineering and Applied Science
Northwestern University, Evanston, IL, 2015

AUTHOR'S NOTE

I decided to write this book for three reasons. First, I believe that entrepreneurship drives human growth and freedom, not large institutions. Individuals, working in small teams, can accomplish miracles. Second, in both my classes and consulting practice, I have seen and felt people's need to be free and their yearning to do "their" thing, on their own terms. I hope more and more people will heed this inner calling and develop the courage to follow their dreams and embrace entrepreneurship. Finally, the Buddha taught us that we should share our knowledge. My love for teaching, mentoring and helping, is my way of passing on everything I have learned. My schedule, unfortunately, only allows me to teach 50 students a year. This book is my way of reaching out to people like you, who have the desire to learn, to search within, to grow and to change the world for the better. We may never meet in person, but our lives may be linked forever.

A Brief History of Entrepreneurship

For most of our existence, humans have lived a meager existence, often on the brink of starvation, ravaged by disease and with short life spans. *The real driver of economic growth and change has been free trade and entrepreneurship.*

Consider the following: For the last several thousand years, the spending power, per person, *per year* (GNP/capita /year) was only about $300 in today's dollars, about the price of *one* fancy meal for you and a friend. People did not travel much - in many cases no more than 30 miles from their village in an entire lifetime.

Then, starting in the early nineteenth century, the economic growth of the world started to take off. Martin Wolf[1], in his book *"Why Globalization Works"* has some wonderful insights and facts. From 1820 – 1998, the economies of the world grew by *900% in real terms, that is by nine times* (9X). Thousands of years of virtually no growth were followed by a "Big Economic Bang."

The driver for this economic explosion was the advent of the industrial revolution. But even as the world economies in aggregate grew by 9X, some economies – mainly the US and Europe - grew even faster by 19X, while a significant part of the world grew by only 6X. What accounted for the difference in these rates? Very simply, the countries that encouraged free trade and entrepreneurial behavior – as opposed to top down, governmental controls – fared much better.

This phenomenon can perhaps be more readily seen from the recent histories of China and India. Forty years ago, both these countries were vastly under-developed and very poor. Their strong growth over the last few decades is a direct result of their governments moving away from socialism and communism and embracing freer trade and entrepreneurship.

Do you want to change the world? Do you want to help solve problems big and small, be it from delivering the basic needs in many poor countries, to better protecting the environment globally, to developing new healthcare models in the Western world? Or maybe you just want to create a new series of books, music, or movies?

Either way, entrepreneurship is the answer.

The Birth Of This Book

I am neither a 27-year-old billionaire who has discovered the magic potion, nor an academic who has spent a lifetime unraveling the mysteries of entrepreneurship. So, why am I writing this book? Bear with me as I share a bit of my story.

I came to the United States when I was 22-years-old, many moons ago. Upon graduating, my intent was to work for a good company for the rest of my life as my father had done in India. I worked for a great company for 20 years and rose to the top levels. In the process I had the privilege to lead wonderful businesses like Rice-A-Roni,

---

[1] Wolf, Martin. *Why Globalization Works*. New Haven: Yale University Press, 2004.

Ghirardelli Chocolate, Quaker Oatmeal, Cap'n Crunch and Aunt Jemima. I was happy and blessed with all the opportunities that came my way.

During this period, while living in the Bay Area for a few years, I was exposed to the Young President's Organization (YPO) - a group whose members had become presidents of large businesses at a young age. Here I found people not only like myself, but also a new breed of people called entrepreneurs. They had started their own companies, had their own vision, hired people they believed in and pretty much ran their own show. The thought of doing things on my own terms, with my own values and beliefs, resonated with me.

A few years later, a colleague and I embarked on a new journey by buying a franchise for a coffee business and starting from scratch. I went from being in charge of billions of dollars, thousands of people and big corporate expense accounts, to a company with zero sales. MBAs were replaced with people who had sometimes barely finished high school. An occasional ride in the corporate plane was replaced with more frequent rides in our coffee trucks. Was I afraid? Of course I was. I wondered if I had made a huge mistake. Had my ego overwhelmed my common sense? I worried if I had borrowed too much money. I was unsure if we would be able to grow the company and I feared looking like a fool.

Mainly, though, I relished the freedom. I liked being in charge of my destiny. We tried many things and made many mistakes, but we changed direction rapidly when needed. We gave our people freedom to please the customers. We treated our people like human beings. We gave them responsibility, but also held them accountable. We grew from zero to a few million dollars in sales. After eight years we sensed a change in the market and sold the company at a very attractive price.

Since then I have run another company and have also started a consulting practice. About twelve years ago, almost on a dare, I decided to teach a class that I had created. Before I knew it, I was *hooked*! I still get "opening night" jitters at the start of each semester. The real reason to teach, it is said, is to learn. I first learn when I prepare for a class and then I learn again when questions and new ideas emerge in the class. Somewhere in this journey I discovered a new passion: to help young people look within and discover their passion, potential and possibly their life's calling.

For the last several years, I have been an Adjunct Faculty Member teaching Northwestern University undergraduates two courses - *"Principles of Entrepreneurship"* and *"Leadership, Ethics and You."*

No, these classes do not make a student an entrepreneur or an ethical leader. Rather they open their mind to possibilities. The knowledge they gain is important. But it is the journey within, that some of them are willing to take, that really excites me and gives me a purpose in life. Watching them grapple with questions such as what they want to do with their lives, how they want to do it and sometimes actually doing it, is truly fulfilling. I believe the real job of a teacher is to help students discover the immense potential that lies within them.

"Everyone has inside of him a piece of good news. The good news is that you don't know how great you can be! How much you can love! What you can accomplish! And what your potential is!" - Anne Frank

Finally, while there are many good books on entrepreneurship, I wanted to write one that demystified and broadened the notions of the subject. Each chapter represents a necessary step towards achieving your final goal of getting a business off the ground. Using this same process in class, I have seen students from all disciplines come alive when they realize that they too can become entrepreneurs and live a meaningful life.

Dream big, work hard, embrace the challenge. A fulfilling and rewarding journey awaits.

Respectfully,

Verinder K. Syal
September 2015

ACKNOWLEDGMENTS

I have been helped by many people in my life, but the limitations of space necessitate that only a few be mentioned by name.

First and foremost, I want to thank my parents. Thanks Mom and Dad for having the courage and foresight to send me to the United States to study 46 years ago. I think you would be proud of this book.

I am thankful for having had many wonderful students in my classes from whom I have learned so much. You know who you are.

I am grateful to Northwestern University, especially The Farley Center for Entrepreneurship and Innovation and the Business Institutions Program, where I have taught for several years. I particularly want to thank Mike Marasco, Mark Witte, Lucy Millman, and Patty Fitzgibbons, for their help and support. I also want to thank two of my friends from Loyola University – Professors Gretchen Dobie and Mike Welch, as well as all the other guest speakers for all that they do for my students.

I want to thank my wife, Leia, for her unflagging support for my students and for letting me spend countless hours working on my classes and this book, without reprimanding me for all the missed social engagements.

Several people gave me insightful feedback. In addition, Steve Fiffer provided valuable editorial feedback, Lisa Panzarella proofread the book meticulously and Chris Bomm formatted the book for publication. Finally, there was a core team of people who worked on this project with me for more than a year. If it reads well, they should receive much of the credit. Any shortcomings are solely mine since I did all the writing and made all the final decisions. Let me start with Roopa Kochhar, my associate in India, who has been with me from the start, through all the versions, sharing her insights and experiences, all the while meticulously ensuring that the final product met her high standards. Vicki Syal, who also happens to be my daughter and a writer in her own right. gave me a clearer perspective and tone for approaching this book. Arabella Watters, a past student of mine, helped with the editing. Finally, I want to thank Liz Gabel for her support and creativity.

I hope this book will persuade you to jump into the entrepreneurial waters and live life on your own terms.

Verinder K. Syal
September 2015
Updated, September, 2017

INTRODUCTION

"Your time is limited, so don't waste it living someone else's life. Don't be trapped by dogma – which is living with the results of other people's thinking. Don't let the noise of other's opinions drown out your own inner voice. And most important, have the courage to follow your heart and intuition. They somehow already know what you truly want to become. Everything else is secondary." - Steve Jobs

"Twenty years from now you will be more disappointed by the things that you didn't do than by the ones you did do. So throw off the bowlines. Sail away from the safe harbor. Catch the trade winds in your sails. Explore. Dream. Discover." - Mark Twain

"The critical ingredient is getting off your butt and doing something. It's as simple as that. A lot of people have ideas, but there are few who decide to do something about them now. Not tomorrow. Not next week. But today. The true entrepreneur is a doer, not a dreamer." - Nolan Bushnell

The Entrepreneurial Revolution

You tap your fingers impatiently: The Wi-Fi is horrific; you know you are running late, but you can't resist uploading this Instagram of your best friend's puppy. The potential "Likes" are just too good to resist. The traffic looks brutal on Waze, so you text your friends. The new tapas place you're going for dinner is supposed to be fantastic. Your two roommates from college are close to launching a new clothing company combining their flair for designing clothes, with a manufacturer they've located in Asia and you're excited to hear about their progress.

You are happy for your friends. They always seem to be doing something different, creative and adventurous (they went skydiving last weekend), have a nice apartment and appear to make a good living. You like their lifestyle and there it is again, the thought that's been gnawing at you for some time: *"Could entrepreneurship be for me too?"*

Such a choice was not always the case. Only a few decades ago, most people worked for one organization all their lives. Today that would be highly unusual. You will probably have 10-20 work experiences in your lifetime. The notion of an early retirement will be a faint memory of a bygone era.

The entrepreneurial revolution kicked into high gear thirty years ago when the Internet became widely available and China, India, Philippines and many countries in Eastern Europe started to embrace free trade and the benefits of globalization. We have come so far, so fast, that it is worth reminding ourselves that Google and the reincarnated Apple, are less than 20 years old. Facebook, Twitter, Airbnb and Uber are of more recent vintage. The Apple App Store, started in 2008, today offers more than a million apps. The rate of change is breathtaking with thousands of new businesses seemingly sprouting up every nanosecond.

I meet many people who are seeking meaning and fulfillment in all aspects of their lives, willing to give up "job security" for the possibility of following their passion. I suspect many of you feel this way too. Your experiences have been different from those of your parents. You have a greater sense of adventure and you like to travel. You love experiencing food, music and ideas from a plethora of cultures. You have the talent and enthusiasm to collaborate with people from every corner of the globe, the capacity to influence customers through social media and the ability to deliver goods speedily and inexpensively, all of which give rise to many opportunities. If anything, the array of choices is overwhelming. The starting lines from *A Tale of Two Cities*[2] capture this dichotomy perfectly: *"It was the best of times, it was the worst of times…"*

---

[2] Dickens, Charles. *A Tale of Two Cities*. London: Chapman & Hall, 1859.

Money, once a limiting factor, is now far more accessible from a variety of sources. Kickstarter, the consummate crowdsourcing site is one of many such examples. Their website offers the following statistics: *"Since our launch on April 28, 2009, over $1 billion has been pledged by more than 7 million people, funding more than 77,000 creative projects."* Projects are classified into 15 categories from art to technology and from fashion to dance. There is something to whet everyone's appetite. One of their biggest successes has been "The Pebble: An E-Paper Watch" which raised more than $10 million.

Besides Crowdsourcing, funds can be raised from friends and family, grants, angel investors and venture capitalists. Suffice to say that virtually every form of creativity and value creation, if it makes business sense (and sometimes even if it does not), appears to have backers.

Another trend favoring entrepreneurship is the dawning realization that large monolithic, bureaucratic organizations can stifle the creativity of their people with their mindless rules and regulations. Schumpeter's "creative destruction" starts as a revolt against this soul stultifying, value destroying, ecosphere. It beckons entrepreneurs to take on these big, rigid, smug dinosaurs. Apple started life taking on IBM while Amazon is challenging all forms of retailing. Skype made communicating with everyone easy and free. Google and Facebook are changing the advertising industry while Uber is revolutionizing personal transportation.

If all these trends are pointing towards entrepreneurship, why are we all not rushing to the promised land of entrepreneurship? *Why are you still wondering? Why have you not jumped into the fray?*

The most likely reason is *fear*. Fear of the unknown. Fear of risk. Fear of failure. Fear of not being good enough. Fear of not being creative. Fear that your idea will be laughed at. Fear of making the wrong choice. Fear of losing what you currently have. Fear of fear.

Are you the only one with this fear? No, this is called the human condition.

If you take the plunge, is success assured? Of course not. No one can guarantee success. But factors such as hard work, commitment, vision, discipline and an intense desire to create something, do increase the probability of success. Entrepreneurship is a process and can be learned and practiced. Peter Drucker, the great thinker and teacher, put it thus:

> *"Entrepreneurship is neither a science nor an art. It is a practice…. Everyone who can face up to decision-making can learn to be an entrepreneur… Entrepreneurship, then, is behavior rather than a personality trait. And it's foundation lies in concept and theory rather than intuition."*

Is there an entrepreneur lurking within you waiting to be freed? Is there an Instagram, WhatsApp, Snapchat, Slack, Nest, SpaceX, Warby Parker, or Kiva somewhere deep down there? Perhaps it is something more personal - a novel, maybe even a trilogy that demands to be given birth. Or, it is a screenplay or movie that you must produce.

Whatever it might be, I am glad you are here.
And, while this book is written as if I am talking to my young students, it is meant for people of all ages.

The journey of a thousand miles starts with a single step.
Welcome to your first step.

How does one start a company? What are the building blocks? How do you come up with a new idea? How do you work well as a team? How do you market and sell? Where will the money come from? How will you make a living? The questions are almost endless. Our goal will be to answer the key questions in an easy to understand way.

Still, this addresses only half the equation of life: "How to make a living?" Is not the more important part of the equation: "How will I live my life?" So many young people talk and think about changing the world, but the change they have in mind often focuses on changing others. It is worth reminding ourselves of Gandhi's advice:

> *"Be the change you wish to see in the world."*

We will therefore explore not only the key elements of entrepreneurship, but will also take time to look within, to ponder on things such as success, happiness and how to live a life of purpose and meaning.

The Design of the Workbook

Each chapter in this book could easily be, and most likely is, a book unto itself. Therefore, this book, just like my classes, has been designed to focus on only the *essence* of each subject. Theory and jargon have been kept to an absolute minimum. I will act as your coach and teach you the fundamentals. It will be your job to dig deeper when the need arises.

When in doubt, focus on the simple, the basic, the essential. Do not get side tracked by the complex, the gaudy and the ephemeral. Remember Einstein's five ascending levels of intelligence:

1. Smart   2. Intelligent   3. Brilliant   4. Genius   5. <u>Simple</u>

There are exercises in almost every chapter. Be sure to do each one and collect your ideas in this book, in one place, and see and feel the progress you are making. The goal of this book is to: 1) help you launch your business and 2) help you look within and define what you want from your life and how you will live it. The following mind map provides a good overview of how the book is laid out

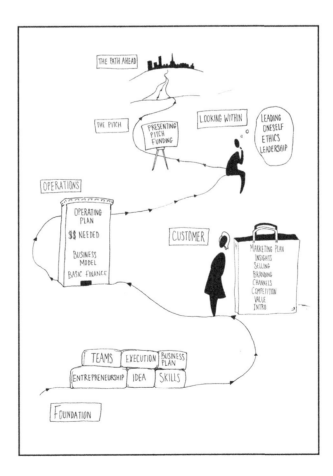

1. **The Foundation**: We will start by defining entrepreneurship - what it is and what it is not. You will then develop a list of ideas that appeal to you and pick one to explore in greater depth. You will learn what skills are needed, why entrepreneurship is better done as a team, how to form a team and how to organize the team to execute successfully. You will then briefly explore what a business model looks like and how it can be best used.

2. **Refining Your Idea - Customer Focus:** In this segment you will take your business idea and refine its customer focus. Without a customer, there is no business. You will learn how to understand your customer, the problem you are solving for them, or a need that you are meeting of theirs. You will learn how to look at an industry, its segments and the competition. You will then determine how you will differentiate your offering, price it, position it and brand it. You will also determine your channels of distribution and develop a sales strategy. By the end of this segment you will have developed a workable marketing plan.

3. **Refining Your Operating Model:** Next you will focus on the profit margins and structure of your business. Can your pricing and margins be improved? Do you have the right operating structure for the level of service you want to provide? You will examine other businesses and develop ideas to refine your business model. You will then determine how much investment is needed to launch your business and develop a 3-year financial forecast.

4. **Looking Within:** We suggest that you explore this segment much sooner, *maybe even start here*. You will think about what leadership really is and why leading oneself is perhaps the hardest thing to do. You will be challenged to develop your values and principles that will lead you not only through your business journey, but also very possibly through your life. You will ask yourself what happiness is and how you plan to live a meaningful life.

5. **The Pitch:** You will now have enough data and ideas to assemble a 10-page business plan and a 10-slide presentation to "pitch" your business to your external and internal constituencies. You will also decide how you will fund your business.

6. **Stepping Out**: This section is brief. You have all the knowledge you need and you will have done all the work necessary to get started. We will remind you of a few simple "rules of the road for the journey" and wish you bon voyage.

Note: We will use the generic "he" throughout the book to make it read consistently. You can substitute it with the word "she" whenever you want.

Replicating the Class

In class we interact extensively. The students have many assignments that are designed to lead them through the process, step by step. Similarly, each chapter of the book will contain an assignment, which you will have to do without my being there to cajole, coax, or grade you. This part of the journey you will have to do with your team.

Let me tell you why the students in my class end up doing a prodigious amount of work, usually voluntarily. In the very first class, we develop a class contract which I call *The Five Accountabilities*. The students define five things they will hold themselves, as individuals, responsible for; five things that the class will hold itself, as a community, responsible for; and five things they want from the professor.

What are the five things that *you* will hold yourself responsible for? (Hint: Here are some things the students generally come up with – put 110% into it, challenge your comfort zone, stay true to yourself, be honest with yourself and be open to constructive criticism. Feel free to add new things to your list.)

Some of the things the students ask of me are: share your experiences, be vulnerable, lead by example, set clear expectations, etc. Even though I will not be in the same physical space as you, here is what I commit to you. This book is as comprehensive, compelling and simple as I can make it to be. I have involved some of my students, and other young people, to get feedback so I could make it even more relevant to you. It has in it all the knowledge that I have accumulated. I believe it also has the key pieces to help you get started.

Holding yourself and your teammates accountable will be the fundamental building block to your success.

Are You Ready?

Michelangelo stated: "Every block of stone has a statue inside it and it is the task of the sculptor to uncover it."
Do you want to uncover this statue within?
Do you want to *Discover The Entrepreneur Within?*

Peter Drucker proclaimed:
"They (Entrepreneurs) achieve what Jefferson hoped to achieve through revolution in every generation, and they do so without bloodshed, civil war, or concentration camps, without economic catastrophe, but with purpose, with direction, and under control."

My question to you is very simple:
Are you up for a bit of a personal revolution?
Personal revolution to achieve freedom.
Freedom to do what you love and to do so on your own terms.
And to help those whose lives you touch.
And to do all this while living a life of meaning and significance.

I believe you are. So, let's get started!

Part I

FOUNDATION

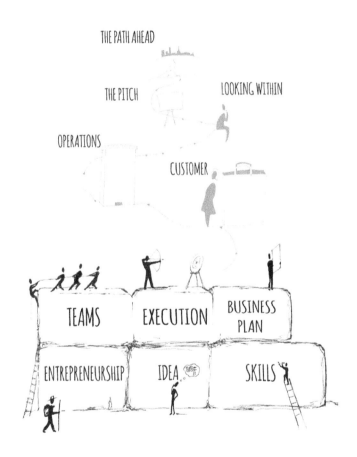

A solid foundation lets you build a tall and long lasting edifice. This first segment is similarly designed to provide you with the foundation to build a strong business. You will learn a new definition of entrepreneurship, generate your starting idea, assess what skills will be needed and get a clear sense of what makes a good team. You will then develop a framework to execute successfully and be introduced to the workings of a business plan.

Chapter 1

WHAT IS ENTREPRENEURSHIP?

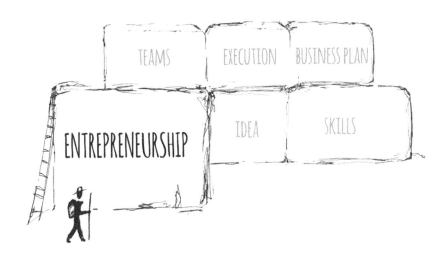

"I can honestly say that I have never gone into any business purely to make money. If that is the sole motive then I believe you are better off not doing it. A business has to be involving, it has to be fun, and it has to exercise your creative instincts." - Richard Branson, Losing My Virginity: How I've Survived, Had Fun, and Made a Fortune Doing Business My Way

"The way to get started is to quit talking and begin doing." - Walt Disney

"When confronted with freedom, we make up things to be afraid of, we invent threats, we seek out things that might go wrong, all so we can avoid the fear of failure, all so we can push ourselves away from the opportunities right in front of us." - Seth Godin, What To Do When It's Your Turn

~~~~~~~~

Key Topics in this Chapter

- Common Definition of Entrepreneur

- Entrepreneurship Redefined

- Common Fears

- Common Myths

- Entrepreneurship is Everywhere

- Where will you find your ideas?

- Assignment: Get Started

Common Definition of Entrepreneur

Ask someone to describe an entrepreneur and you are likely to hear something like this: a person who creates businesses, works insane hours, takes great risks, hocks everything he has, and sometimes becomes very rich, and at other times goes broke. Run the movie a bit longer and you will catch glimpses of young, beautiful people living in desirable places, sharing insights to rival the Greek philosophers and having lifestyles that would make Cleopatra envious.

Perhaps I exaggerate. But just a smidgen. Like most myths, there is a hint of truth to such images combined with a fair bit of smoke. It is true that an entrepreneur does start an enterprise with considerable initiative and hard work. Is taking huge risks a necessary condition for entrepreneurship? We don't think so. As for their wit, wisdom, looks and lifestyle, we'll just say "no comment."

Another common misconception is that entrepreneurship and technology are synonymous and this creative world is restricted to Silicon Valley. The media extol the glamorous stories about Apple, Facebook, Google, Instagram, Snapchat, or a WhatsApp, in part because it is far more fun visiting California than Cleveland. In reality, technology is being created all over the world. Furthermore, technology is only a part, actually a small part, of the entrepreneurial revolution. In the United States, technology accounts for less than 2% of the economy. The application of technology, however, may be a far greater wealth creator.

Just as there is a real world beyond Hollywood, the real world of entrepreneurship is not limited to a tiny sliver of California. You can start your revolution from anywhere in the world, including Cleveland. You do not have to be a technology wiz to start your journey.

Entrepreneurship Redefined

Fundamentally, entrepreneurs are problem solvers. *They identify problems and instead of complaining about them, they ask, "What is the solution? How can this be fixed, changed, or done better?"*

Peter Drucker[3], in his classic book *Innovation and Entrepreneurship*, defined entrepreneurship as follows:

"Entrepreneurship is neither a science nor an art. It is a practice….
Innovation is the specific tool of entrepreneurs, the means by which they exploit change as an opportunity for a different business or a different service… Entrepreneurs innovate.
It is the act that endows resources with a new capacity to create wealth."

He further added:

"Everyone who can face up to decision-making can learn to be an entrepreneur…Entrepreneurship, then, is behavior rather than a personality trait. And its foundation lies in concept and theory rather than intuition."

While these thoughts challenge conventional wisdom, take that as a good sign since conventional wisdom is often wrong. Let's examine these insights again:

- Entrepreneurship is neither a science nor an art. It is a *practice*.
- Everyone who can face up to *decision-making* can learn to be an entrepreneur.
- Entrepreneurship, then, is *behavior* rather than a personality trait.
- *Innovation* is the specific tool of entrepreneurs, the means by which they exploit change as an opportunity for a different business or a different service.

---

[3] Drucker, Peter. *Innovation and Entrepreneurship*. New York: HarperBusiness, 1985.

- Entrepreneurship, when done right, *reduces risk*.

Most people never start on this entrepreneurial path because they believe that "successful" entrepreneurs have "it," whatever "it" might be, while they do not. They think of entrepreneurs as an alien race kissed by the gods. They imagine this super race receiving text messages from the heavens proclaiming "Facebook, that's it my son! Too late for that? Try WhatsApp. Again, too late? Really? Oh well, then how about Snapchat? Don't tell me that the image has already disappeared?"

Relax. Entrepreneurs are not some incarnation of an evolved species. Entrepreneurship is a process. If you are willing to learn this process and embrace the discipline, you will give yourself a good chance to succeed.

Look for problems to be solved. Look for change that is happening around you, because change signals opportunity. All the pieces you need are often right in front of you. Sometimes you just have to assemble these pieces in a different way.

Let's examine some examples:

- Hamburgers had been sold for a few millennia, but it was Ray Kroc who brought new value to McDonald's by developing standardization of the products, production and service. This then endowed the same resources – meat, potatoes and the like - with considerable wealth generating capacity. Given the focus on eating healthier and the concern with obesity across the globe, it appears that McDonald's will have to reinvent itself again.
- Walmart revolutionized the world and added considerable economic value by developing and fine-tuning what we now call the "supply chain." At its core, supply chain is about becoming more efficient by eliminating unnecessary steps in a process. Ikea is another example of rethinking the entire process from conception to sale. All industries across the world have adopted many of these practices, thereby reducing inefficiency and creating wealth.
- Amazon challenged the book publishing and distribution industry and is now taking on just about every other retailer on the planet.
- Apple has made a considerable dent in the oligopolies of the music and telephony industries and Netflix is doing the same with the television industry.
- Skype has obsoleted the long distance telephone monopolies.
- Grameen Bank brought microfinance and economic growth to the poor in Bangladesh by looking at things afresh.
- Zipcar offered an alternative for city dwellers to owning cars.
- Uber is taking this further and revolutionizing personal travel while turning the traditional taxi model on its head.

Notice that in most cases technology was not the driver but only a component. It was the ability to rethink the existing processes that led to many of these new products and services.

New ideas engender new solutions, which invariably destroy the status quo. In a 2012 article in *The Wall Street Journal*, Andy Kessler passionately explains how entrepreneurs, following Schumpeter's dictum of creative destruction, create many, many jobs even as they destroy existing businesses. "Apple employs just 47,000 people and Google under 25,000. Like Staples, they have destroyed many old jobs...But by lowering the cost of doing business they've enabled innumerable entrepreneurs to start new businesses and employ hundreds of thousands, even millions, of workers worldwide - all while capital gets re-deployed more effectively."

You are probably thinking that this is fine for large organizations, but how does this apply to me, a one-person marching band? Everything starts off small. Many of the well-known entrepreneurs did not even finish college - Gates, Jobs, Dell, Zuckerberg, Branson - and some of their initial ideas started in dorm rooms. It is the passion, desire and need from within to do something that allows people to start this journey.

You might be wondering how entrepreneurship is different from starting any business. It's a good question that requires some digging into.

Assume you are thinking of opening a pizzeria in a district full of restaurants, including two pizza places. You are opening the pizzeria because it has been your life-long dream to own a restaurant. You feel that not only can you make better pizza than anybody else, but you'll also be able to run the place more efficiently, essentially by outworking everybody. Your spirit is undoubtedly commendable but let's examine the logic.

First of all, you must ask yourself what problem are you solving? Does the area need another restaurant? Not really – after all, there are already several restaurants there.

Does the area need another pizza restaurant? There are two existing pizza places currently. What problem would you be solving, or what new delight do you plan to offer?

If you don't have answers to these questions, then the business is not only risky, but it's quite possibly not a good idea. Suffice to say, *it is also not entrepreneurship*. After all, entrepreneurship demands that either a problem be solved or a new delight be created.

Now let's assume that you have done your research and found that people in that particular area are bored with the pizzas that are available. They would like a greater variety of crusts, toppings and perhaps meatless or gluten-free options. Also in demand is a wider selection of craft beers to accompany the meal and, because you are near a university town, they would like late night delivery, which is currently not available. *Now you are solving potential problems and thinking more like an entrepreneur.*

Then you would look at several other factors such as the team, location, lease, capital needed and the returns that investors would require. You would think of pricing, profits and develop a rudimentary cash flow forecast. You would do this thinking and research *before* you decided to sign a lease and launch. *This is how you reduce risk.*

This type of pre-strategizing sometimes scares people because they are afraid that their precious idea won't make the cut. However, it is this very forethought that can lead to modifying an idea for the better, or if the idea is not feasible, it can potentially save a whole lot of trouble, time and money.

Common Fears

The first session of our entrepreneurship class is always memorable. Visualize 25 students, bright, fresh and eager to learn. A few fancy themselves as entrepreneurs and are not sure why they are even taking this class, other than the fact that a friend has told them "this was *the* class to take." Some have come to see what this thing called entrepreneurship ("How do you spell it by the way?") is all about, but are quite certain that it's *not* for them. Then there are others who have already decided that they do not want to work for "soulless monolithic giants." Amidst their excitement, a palpable sense of fear is discernible.

I ask them what are they most afraid of? I sense their angst and doubts as to whether they can succeed. In rapid fire I hear:

- I am not creative.
- I am not an engineer.
- I do not know anybody. I have no network. I hate every single one of my Facebook friends!
- I never have any really brilliant ideas.
- I have a lot of great ideas, but I do not know where to start.
- I never finish anything I start.
- I have no money.
- I have no time.
- I'd like to give it a try, but I am just too risk averse.
- I'd love to, but I don't think I can.
- What will people (my parents, friends) think or say?

The list is almost endless. Does any of this sound familiar to you? Do you have any of these doubts? It would not be human to not have some of these doubts. I have had these doubts as well. So, how do we confront them? We will examine them one at a time and understand what the problem really is and see whether we can develop a solution. Let's don our "entrepreneurial hats" and lift this cloud of darkness.

- *I am not creative:* Actually, most of us have a fair bit of creativity. We just don't tap into it often. Why not watch a couple of TED videos - *"Your Elusive Creative Genius"* by Elizabeth Gilbert and *"How to live before you die"* by Steve Jobs - to get your juices going? Furthermore, entrepreneurship is a team sport. Perhaps someone else on your team will be the creative spark plug. You do not need to do everything.
- *I am not an engineer:* It turns out that engineers are about 2% of the U.S. workforce. Most of you will not be engineers. That is why you need a team.
- *I do not know anybody. I have no network:* We mistake the superficiality of social media interaction for having, or not having, friends. I once challenged a student to make a list of people whom she could call at any time for help. The list turned out to be far more extensive than she had imagined. Everyone has a network - big or small. It just has to be nourished and sometimes rejuvenated.
- *I never have any really brilliant ideas:* If this is the case, find friends who do. Entrepreneurship is more than just about brilliant ideas. An idea without execution is meaningless. Sometimes the ability to complete things may be the more pressing talent a business needs.
- *I have a lot of great ideas but I do not know where to start:* This book will provide you with a model to starting and completing tasks.
- *I never finish anything I start:* You are going to have to learn and commit to doing so, or you will let your team and yourself down. Start first by finishing this book!
- *I have no money:* There are many new options now, including crowdfunding.
- *I have no time:* All of us have 24 hours in a day. What we do with those 24 hours is what can make or break us. We all waste time. I know I waste time catching up with the news more frequently than needed. Could you find a couple of hours of time for yourself in a day? I think most people can, if it is important enough to them.
- *I'd like to give it a try but I am just too risk averse:* We are all genetically programmed differently. But what if entrepreneurship is not as risky as you think? Everything in life entails some risk, even crossing the street. I challenge you to reexamine your risk preference.
- *I'd love to but I don't think I can:* Henry Ford said, *"Whether you think you can, or you think you can't - you're right."* Most of us limit ourselves with our beliefs. How about you?
- *What will people (my parents, friends) think or say?:* We will examine some of these questions in a later chapter. For now, ask yourself, whose life is this anyway?

This thought experiment was not meant to be glib; rather it was designed to help you think from a different perspective. We all have doubts and fears. The human brain is wired to worry. How do we surmount our fears? By finding solutions while also trying to understand ourselves. The reality is that the vast majority of the problems that we worry about never come to pass. To be paralyzed or not to be paralyzed is our choice.

Not living is not an option. Could working hard, being persistent, resilient and embracing life with passion be a better answer?

Common Myths

Some of the more common myths are:

- Entrepreneurs are born - one cannot learn to become an entrepreneur.
- Entrepreneurs take huge risks.
- I have to do it alone.
- I have to have a large network.
- I must have a big idea.
- I must be lucky or a real genius to come up with a big idea.
- I need a lot of money to get started.

- Silicon Valley is where all entrepreneurship takes place.
- I have to be charismatic.

How many of these fears and myths are accurate? *Not many. Perhaps none of them are.*

Entrepreneurship can be learned and if done right, you will reduce some of the risk before you embark on something. You don't need to do things alone. Form a team and divide the work and leverage each other's strengths. It is strange how luck seems to favor hard work. Also, you do not need to move anywhere to get started. If charisma is not your strong suit, be thankful.

A myth is a story often involving supernatural forces. It is generally a widely held belief that is not true. How then do we dispel our fears and myths? We wake up and take action.

Entrepreneurship is Everywhere!

Undoubtedly there is a lot of energy, excitement and buzz around things that come out of Silicon Valley. *The Wall Street Journal* published an infographic in 2015 depicting the 73 companies globally valued at over $1 billion. Yes, admittedly, tech unicorns like Uber ($41.2 billion) and Palantir ($15 billion) were in the upper echelons with possibly inflated valuations. But there were several non-tech companies too, such as a consumer good company - Honest Co., ($1 billion), a healthcare company - Theranos ($9 billion) and a real estate company - WeWork ($5 billion).

Silicon Valley has been the center of a great technological revolution. The tech valuations do sometimes defy imagination and their successes are not always easy to replicate. None of this is meant to diminish what is happening in Silicon Valley, rather it is meant to assert that entrepreneurship is possible everywhere in every industry. Furthermore, businesses that tend to make money, rather than just hoping to make money, are more sustainable. So where should *you* look? Everywhere.

To help my students understand the breadth of possibilities, I have them read Rachel Bridge's[4] *My Big Idea* which highlights 30 small entrepreneurial ventures across a variety of industries in the UK. Examples include companies offering hot dogs, coffee, baby foods, insurance, travel a computer service. There is even the story of the young lady who convinced the musical group Abba to support her idea of making the musical *Mama Mia*. Where did all these ideas come from? Often they arose from their passions, their life circumstances and their travels. The students breathe a sigh of relief because these are stories they can relate to and they can see themselves doing similar things.

To dispel the myth of "only Silicon Valley," my friend and entrepreneur, Robert Jordan[5] researched 45 entrepreneurs from technology and non-technology companies in the Midwest, who had created $41 billion of value. Based on their stories, he wrote *How They Did It: Billion Dollar Insights from the Heart of America* - a book that you may want to read for both ideas and inspiration.

An excerpt: *"Founder Joe Mansueto shares how he started Morningstar in his apartment in Chicago Illinois and grew the company to serve 7 million customers. Raj Soin talks about founding MTC with $1,700 in Columbus Ohio, surviving without cash and eventually selling to BAE for $425 million. Rock Mackie, founder of TomoTherapy in Madison Wisconsin, had to lay off all his employees at launch but eventually went on to a billion-dollar IPO."*

I do not want to minimize the great benefits created by Silicon Valley type companies; they have generated enormous value and in many cases changed the way we live. But I do want to emphasize the fact that there are many ways to create value, in virtually every industry and in every country. Create a technology company if that is your passion, but using technology as a driver may open up even more opportunities.

Problem – Solution, that is the real mantra of entrepreneurs. Understand the process, develop the discipline and see how your world changes.

---

[4] Bridge, Rachel. *My Big Idea*. Philadelphia: Kogan Page Limited, 2006.

[5] Jordan, Robert. *How They Did It: Billion Dollar Insights from the Heart of America*. Redflash Press, 2010.

Where Will You Find Your Ideas?

Ideas are all around us. Often they are within us, but we do not see them. How then do we develop a systematic way of collecting ideas? It starts with the mindset.

The Mindset: Don't get annoyed, smile.

Entrepreneurs are problem solvers. Therefore, you need to start looking at the world with a new set of eyes and developing a new thought process. Every time something does not seem right - be it a product you have bought or a service that has been unsatisfactory - instead of getting annoyed, smile. You have just been handed a gift. You have encountered a problem that may require a solution, which has in it the seeds of a possible business. Given the craziness and ineptness of the world at large, you may find yourself smiling a lot.

Tina Seelig[6] in her book: *What I wish I knew when I was 20*, has the following suggestions to expand your mindset:
- Take off your blinders.
- See problems afresh.
- Question all rules.
- Don't wait to be asked.
- Give yourself permission.
- Failure is not fatal. This is the secret sauce of Silicon Valley.

Seth Godin[7], the author of *Purple Cow* in a blog post observed:
- Ideas occur when dissimilar universes collide.
- Ideas fear experts, but they adore a beginner's mind.
- Ideas come from nature.
- Ideas don't need a passport.
- Ideas hate conference rooms, particularly where there is a history of criticism.

This then is the mindset of the entrepreneur that you must embrace. You must give yourself permission to think and act differently and be open to ideas and thoughts from everywhere.

The Search For Ideas

I suspect you already have a few ideas. Let me suggest ten ways to add to your list, by looking at both things in your personal life as well as looking at the "Big Picture."

Personal

1. **Frustrations**: Things that frustrate you in your immediate life, where you say to yourself, "Why do they do this or why do they not do this?" I wonder if this is how Zuckerberg started Facebook when he could not get a date? On a less jocular note, Dropbox came about because Drew Houston found himself in a place where he wanted to work, but had forgotten to bring his flash drive containing the files he needed.
2. **Improvements**: There is this app that you use, *all the time,* but something about it always irks you. Maybe you need to develop a new app. If you have such a need, others probably do too. *Babylicious,* a UK

---

[6] Seelig, Tina. *What I wish I knew when I was 20*. New York: HarperCollins Publishers, 2010.
[7] Godin, Seth. *Purple Cow*. New York: Penguin Group US, 2003.

company, was started by a mother who was not satisfied by the convenience of the baby food available. She decided to develop a baby food in the form of ice cubes.

3. **Hobbies**: This is a fertile area. Do you like playing games? Is that how Candy Crush came about? Instagram was a hobby before it became a big business. Do you have a hobby that would enrich the world and you?

4. **Passion**: This drives many of us. What are you passionate about? Photography? Helping the indigent? Scarce water resources? Teaching? Saving the whales? Whatever it might be, what could you do to actually make a difference? Patagonia has combined its passion for the environment with its clothing business. Kiva allows people to provide help to the needy with microloans.

5. **Cross Pollination**: Perhaps you saw something in your travels that you think could be used in your hometown; or you saw an idea on the web that could be applied to another business. Nowadays, ideas float freely across borders. Flipkart is attempting to do in India what Amazon has done in the United States and Europe.

Big Picture

1. **Demographic Trends:** What are some of the key trends you see? There are many, but let's look at a few to get started:
    1. An aging U.S. population: Their needs and wants will be many: healthcare, housing, finances and travel to name just a few. The Baby Boomers may be getting old, but for now, they have a lot of money and can afford many goods and services.
    2. A much more diversified population: Hispanics are now 17% of the population and growing. Asian Americans are now close to 6% and are also one of the most affluent groups in the country. What do these groups need and want? What kind of foods, groceries, restaurants, medicines and health clubs are needed to support their needs and wants?

2. **Perceptions / Beliefs:** Peter Drucker once pointed out that we are living much longer than ever before, but we are also more focused on health as never before. Perceptions and beliefs do not need any mathematical proofs, they just are. The Green movement is strong today. There are people who believe that being a vegetarian or even a vegan is the best diet. Others feel strongly that a low carbohydrate diet is the way to go. Understand that each of these areas is rife for adding value in the form of a product or service.

3. **Things that just don't make sense**: Zipcar found a solution for people who lived in cities and did not need a car very often. iTunes was the answer to not being forced to buy an entire album when you only wanted a few songs. I personally don't care for the TSA at the airports. To my delight, on a recent flight I discovered a new company called Clear (Clearme.com) whose slogan warmed my heart: *"Travel Better. Faster. Smarter. Skip the line and get to your gate in half the time."* As soon as the service becomes available in Chicago, I will sign up. Taxi services in most cities leave much to be desired creating a perfect opening for Uber.

4. **Food and Fashion:** Forty years ago, the only upscale restaurant experience in Chicago was limited to French cuisine. For the more plebeian palate there were two additional choices - Mexican and Chinese. Today, that is certainly not the case. Alinea proclaims that it "combines food with science and art" and NEXT, the spinoff restaurant from executive chef Grant Achatz, which pioneered rotating menus and ticketed dining, are changing the way high-end dining out can be experienced. Stephanie Izard, a past winner of Top Chef, uses her celebrity chef status, and branding chops, to reign supreme over her two Chicago staples, The Girl & The Goat and The Little Goat. This scene is being repeated in many cities, as they become modern meccas for foodies.
    1. On the fashion front, a recent business headline blared *Nasty Gal just raised a $12.7 million round.* Sophie Amaruso was 22 when she started the Nasty Gal store on eBay in her garage to appeal to stylish, young, women who couldn't afford premium fashion labels. The company was

incorporated in 2008 and in six short years, it has grown 10,000 percent. At 22, she saw a problem and offered a solution. Do you see any problems?

5. **Connections:** People are more connected than ever before in the history of the world thanks to Tindr, Yik Yak, WhatsApp, Viber and Facebook. Air travel, made quite affordable by the likes of Southwest, Spirit and Ryan, extends this connectivity even further. Undoubtedly there are still many more opportunities to be developed in this space. At the same time, I believe that technology is making us more self-centered and shy. The last time you were in a restaurant, did you perchance see a table with a group of people texting, checking emails, talking on the phone, all the while being oblivious to their dinner companions? Our favorite mantra may be: "Any place but here, any time but now." Could it be that despite the thousands of friends on Facebook we are lonelier than ever before? Is there a need for ventures focused on real connections?

This list is just to whet your appetite. You are only limited by your imagination.

ASSIGNMENTS – GET STARTED BY ANSWERING THESE QUESTIONS:

How do you define an entrepreneur? What do you think it takes to become one?

What are YOUR fears?

What are some of your myths about entrepreneurship?

Where Will You Find Your Ideas? Here are some suggestions:

What are some things in your daily life that could be improved?

List your hobbies and passions.

Is there something in another country or another industry that could be cross-pollinated?

What are some demographic trends you notice and feel passionate about?

Things that don't make sense.

The Starting List: Look at the ideas above and pick TEN of them for now. Don't overthink it for now.

1.

2.

3.

4.

5.

6.

7.

8.

9.

10.

As you close this chapter, please remember: Problem – Solution, that is the real mantra of entrepreneurs. Understand the process, develop the discipline and see how your world changes.

Additional Notes

Chapter 2

YOUR STARTING IDEA

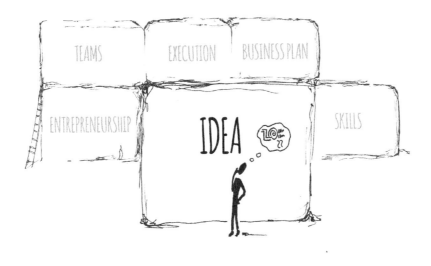

"New things, new ideas arrived and strutted their stuff and were vilified by some and then lo! that which had been a monster was suddenly totally important to the world." - Terry Pratchett, Raising Steam

"The way to get good ideas is to get lots of ideas and throw the bad ones away." - Linus Pauling

"A mediocre idea that generates enthusiasm will go further than a great idea that inspires no one." - Mary Kay Ash

~~~~~~~~

Key Topics in this Chapter

- Ideas Galore

- The Screening Filter

- The End Result: Final Pitch

- Assignment: From Three Ideas to One

Ideas Galore

If you are anything like my students, you and your team have had a great time generating ideas. You have been on a tear. The juices were flowing, bolts of creativity were flashing and new, innovative and sometimes crazy ideas kept popping up as you discussed your passions, likes and dislikes, dreams and aspirations. Sometimes the ideas shifted and changed as you built off of each other.

You may have a sheet or two or more of ideas in front of you. "The game is afoot," as Sherlock Holmes would say.

Like Sherlock, you have to sift through a lot of ideas to find the *one* that is worth digging deeper into. That is what this chapter is designed to do. We will introduce you to *I-BET*, the *Initial Business Evaluation Tool* that will help you sort your ideas.

Warren Buffett, the well known investor and CEO of Berkshire Hathaway, is known to decide within five minutes whether to do a deal or not. He can do this because he has spent a lifetime thinking about what he wants to do, what his competence is, what kind of people he wants to work with and what the financial returns will be. Mr. Buffett is one of a kind, but we can learn from his discipline and approach. With a bit of practice and experience, you too will get good enough to sort through ideas quite rapidly. No time to waste, let's get started.

The Screening Filter

You will need to screen your ideas to settle on your starting idea. They are five filters or steps in *I-BET (Initial Business Evaluation Tool)*. Please note that we will delve into each of these topics in greater detail as we go along. For now, focus on understanding the concepts, so you can go through your list of ideas and settle upon your initial best idea as quickly as possible. (Also, note that there are many ways to do such a screening, be it *Canvas* that is used by Eric Ries' *Lean Startup* adherents, or *Business Model Generation* as enunciated by Alexander Osterwalder & Yves Pigneur, just to name a few. Use the method that works best for you. I have personally found the I-BET screening filter easiest to use.)

Filter 1: Problem / Solution

In most cases, a new business idea is an answer to a problem. Let's look at some well-known businesses and see how they might have conceptualized this problem-solution equation.

- **iTunes**
  - *Problem*
    - *For Music Lovers*: "I have to buy an entire album when all I want is a few tracks. And, boy, are the albums expensive!"
    - *For Record Companies*: "People are downloading for *free* from Napster. If we don't find a better model, we will go out of business."
  - *Solution*: Make each song track available for a nominal price (99 cents). People will be more willing to pay for individual songs. Music companies will get a new revenue stream. Add DRM to the soundtracks to limit piracy.
  - (Aside: Spotify may be the successor to iTunes, replacing the need to buy individual songs with an almost unlimited supply of music for a modest monthly fee.)

- **Southwest Airlines**
  - *Problem (imagine you are in 1967)*: Airline travel is prohibitively expensive. Very few people can afford to fly.
  - *Solution*: Provide an alternative solution for driving 500 miles that is comparable in cost.

- **Google**
    - *Problem*: Advertising is inefficient as captured by this famous quote from John Wanamaker: *"Half my advertising is wasted, I just don't know which half."*
    - *Solution*: Develop a way to target advertising thereby avoiding the waste.

- **Yelp**
    - *Problem*: People are no longer using Yellow Pages to search for purveyors of goods and services. Therefore, companies are reducing their advertising in Yellow Pages.
    - *Solution*: Create an online version since people are now using the web to gather information.

- **Plated**
    - *Problem*: Many busy professionals like cooking gourmet food, but don't have the time to research recipes and shop for ingredients.
    - *Solution*: Provide them everything they will need to cook at home.

- **Instagram**
    - Sometimes offering a delightful experience can result in a large business opportunity. Instagram combined a photo centric app with geotagging capabilities, allowing people to share snippets of their lives in an aesthetically pleasing way. The app was downloaded 100,000 times within a week of its launch. The company was acquired by Facebook 551 days later, before it had made even a single dollar of revenue.

Filter 2: The Product

iTunes: *An online music store* where you can sample the music, buy instantly without having to go to a store.

Southwest Airlines: *A low cost, no frills airline*, based on a new operating model, flying 300-500 miles, with a touch of fun.

Google: *A search engine* having a vast array of knowledge, which becomes the first choice for people to look up information. When people do a search, an ad for related products also appears. This increases the odds that the ad is relevant and that they will click on the link.

YELP: Provide an *online directory of service.* (The business model was later strengthened by creating a platform for crowd-sourced reviews about people's experiences, which then allowed customers to make more informed choices.)

Plated: Provide *a home delivery service that provides* "A weekly box of fresh and seasonal ingredients" for recipes that you have picked or, if you prefer, have been picked for you.

Instagram: An easy, aesthetically pleasing and *social way to share photos.*

Filter 3: Who Is Your Customer?

You will learn to define in greater depth who your customer is in a later chapter. For now, start by thinking about the following questions:

- Who is your customer? (Their demographics such as age, sex, education, income, etc.)
- Why will they buy your product?

- Can you visualize them? Develop an Avatar.

Let's imagine how these companies thought of their customers:

iTunes: At the time of inception, their customers were likely to be in the 15-30 year age bracket, conscious of money with limited allowance - especially for the younger set. While they initially liked Napster and the free downloads, the 99-cent price, huge selection and ease of use offered by iTunes won them over. How about the Avatar? Were you part of iTunes' first customer base?

Southwest Airlines: Who were the customers in 1967? Probably people between the ages of 30 and 60. People who would have driven 300-500 miles but found the airfare attractive. They were not business travelers. They were more likely to be a couple going on a vacation or visiting their families. The Avatar would probably be a 40-year-old couple, middle class, family oriented, with a slight flair for adventure (since flying was uncommon at that time).

Plated: Their slogan is "Eating Well Made Easy." The customers have to be working Millennials, either single or young couples, who eat out quite often and have an income of $75,000-200,000. They also like to dabble in cooking interesting recipes and enjoy having meals at home from time to time. Visualizing them shouldn't take more than a quick look in the mirror for some of you.

Filter 4: Who Is The Competition?
(And What Do You Do Better?)

There is always competition. Sometimes it is direct and other times it is indirect. The sub-title asks you the key question: What will you do better and how? If you are the same as everyone else, it is just a commodity business. Let's take a look at a couple of examples.

Google: 90% of Google's revenues (and even more of its profits) come from selling advertising. Who is its competition? Radio, television and newspapers as a starter. While the first two have held their own to date, newspapers are hurting because they have become an inefficient medium. On the Web, many companies develop models hoping to capture ad dollars. Google reigns supreme because of their algorithms, scale and ecosphere. The coming competition is in mobile and they are getting stiff competition from Facebook. (All this data can be easily researched.)

Southwest Airlines: Initially their competition was cars, more specifically people who would drive the 300-500 mile trips. Today it is all the other airlines including American, United, Delta and JetBlue. What do they do better? Better prices, generally better service and "bags fly free."

Big companies can suck up a lot of oxygen, but they can also be ripe for the "creative destruction" that we have mentioned earlier. A prime example is Blockbuster and Netflix. Blockbuster saw Netflix coming for years, but did nothing about it. They made feeble attempts, but never took Netflix as a serious competitor. The combination of a high fixed cost structure in the form of stores, as well as a dependence on "late fees" killed them, although it was a slow death.

The real lesson is that you cannot rest on your laurels; you must constantly strive to improve your product. If you do not, sooner or later, someone will obsolete you. Netflix has learned this lesson. Therefore, even after achieving considerable success, it continues to push forward with innovation. Using data gathered from their customers' watch lists, they have developed algorithms to determine what their viewers watch the most and have applied this data to develop their own original content such as *House of Cards* and *Orange is the New Black*. However, if I were Netflix, I'd be wary of Amazon and its Prime Video offering.

Filter 5: Will You Make Money?
(What Is Your Business Model?)

A Business Model is a fancy way of answering some basic financial questions, all designed to answer the last question.

- What is your selling price?
- What is your cost?
- What will your sales be in Year 1?
- How much money will you need?
- How long will it take to break-even?
- *Will you make money?*

Let's see if we can understand the Business Models for some of the businesses we have been discussing.

iTunes / Apple: Most songs are sold for 99 cents. This is about what Apple pays to the record labels. Therefore, they make little or no money on this segment of its business. However, iTunes does help Apple sell plenty of iPods, Macs and iPhones, which make handsome profits. Their business model then, is to break even on iTunes and make their money selling hardware. (Amazon on the other hand has the opposite business model. They lose money on the hardware - Kindle, Fire Tablets, Fire Phones, etc. - but make money on the content that customers buy.)

Southwest Airlines: Why has Southwest continued to make money while most airlines have gone through bankruptcies? They have a different business model. They never bought into the hub and spoke model that the other airlines tried for many years and lost money on. Southwest focuses on only one kind of airplane, the Boeing 737. Most other airlines have multiple suppliers, i.e. Boeing and/or Airbus at the very least, with multiple kinds of planes from each supplier. Southwest's business model leads to less complexity and lower operating costs. For example, they can turn around an airplane within 30 minutes of landing, while most other airlines struggle to do so in 60 minutes. This allows them to use their planes more efficiently. All the major US airlines, American, United and Delta, have gone through bankruptcies. In contrast, Southwest has had 41 consecutive years of profitability. Besides a radical business model, great leadership and a people oriented culture have been major contributors to their success.

Plated: We do not have their data but let's take a guess at how their model might work by answering the basic questions:
- *Selling Price:* The website tells us that the selling price starts at $12/plate with each recipe containing two servings/plate. Let's assume that, on average, people buy 4 plates/week at a price of $15/plate, this would make the weekly revenue per customer $60.
- *Cost:* There are three main costs: 1) cost of ingredients, 2) cost of delivery and 3) cost of staff including the chefs that they have on their payroll.
- *Sales* would be estimated by taking the average revenue/week/customer and multiplying it by the number of customers and then multiplying it by 52 weeks.
- Most businesses are likely to run at a loss until they achieve scale. The goal is to keep the costs as low as possible and work to achieve scale as quickly as possible. Plated seems to be achieving scale rapidly. They currently deliver to 95% of the Continental United States from eight locations.
- *Money needed to start up*: It is possible they could have started up with limited capital (we do not know), by outsourcing the picking up of ingredients and the delivery of the meals. They might have rented space and hired staff to package the food.
- *How long before break even?* It's hard to tell. It depends on how fast they want to expand; the faster the expansion, the longer it takes to break even. On a market by market basis, they might be able to break even in perhaps two years

- *Will they make money?* With scale they could be quite profitable. A good restaurant generally makes 10% on every dollar of sales. Generally, the cost of food, real estate and staff is about 30% each for a total cost of 90%. Plated can reach many more customers than a restaurant. Their main costs are that of assembling the recipes and delivering the ingredients. Will their ongoing margins exceed 10%? We would think so.
- We do not have any data for Plated other than what we know from experience and what is on the website. We shared this example to illustrate that the thought process is not complex and requires mostly common sense

Thinking about your business model and how you will make money up front is very important. Making reasonable assumptions at the early stage is quite appropriate. Not thinking about it at all is a *no-no*. When I ran large businesses, I never had to worry about running out of money. When we started our own business, the bankroll was much smaller. Why do some people not address this question at the start? Could it be that they are afraid of the answer?

Entrepreneurship is about reducing risk, not embracing death-defying odds. Having even rough answers can be incredibly liberating.

A caution is in order. The real work will start after you have picked your first idea. You will spend an enormous amount of energy and effort digging deep into all aspects of your proposed business, vetting it from all angles, to maximize your chances of success. You will understand your business better than anyone else. You will be able to explain your concepts to your customers, suppliers, fellow workers and investors with speed, ease and in depth when called for. You will be ready with your *"Final Pitch."* I like to know where I am going and I suspect you do too. Let's take a quick look at what this final output might look like. Otherwise as Yogi Berra said: *"If you don't know where you are going, you might wind up someplace else."* We wouldn't want to end up someplace else.

The End Result: The Final Pitch

Just before you launch, you will need to "pitch" your business to many people. Visualize and embrace the key parts you will have in hand:

1. *An Elevator Pitch:* You will be able to explain to everyone what your idea is in a compelling and engaging manner, in under *60 seconds*.

2. *The Pitch Deck:* You will have a 10-slide, 30-font, presentation deck. These 10 slides will capture the essence of your business. The 30-font requirement forces you to be parsimonious with your words. Use pictures when possible. We recommend the following slides:

   i.   *Problem / Solution:* What is the problem that your product (we use the word product and service interchangeably) is solving? What is the solution you are offering?
   ii. *Product:* Describe your product.
   iii. *Customer:* Who is your customer? Plan to understand your customer better than they understand themselves.
   iv. *Competition:* Who else is offering something similar? Why is your product superior?
   v.   *Marketing and Sales:* How will you market and sell your product?
   vi. *Business Model:* What will your price and cost be? How will you make money?
   vii. *Financial Plan:* 3 Year Financial forecast.
   viii. *Funding:* How much money will you need and how do you plan to fund it?
   ix. *The Team:* Who are you, what are your combined strengths and why are you the best people to make this happen?
   x.   *Timeline:* When do you plan to start and what are the milestones along the growth path?
        The discerning will have noted that the five filters used earlier are among the 10 slides in the Pitch Deck. All the work you will do will lead towards *The Final Pitch*.

3. *An Executive Summary:* A 2-page document summarizing the above points.

4. *A 10-page Business Plan:* This will be the written version of the 10-slide deck. Some people prefer to read, others prefer a conversation. You must be ready for both.

5. *Back Ups:* During the course of researching and compiling your business plan, you will develop a considerable amount of data which will result in a lot of slides and exhibits. As partners, vendors, lenders or investors get more interested they will want to dig deeper into your business. The 10-page slide deck may become 50 slides or even more. The depth of the presentation will depend on the audience.

Does this seem a bit daunting? It can be, but it need not be. Every slide, every idea that you need, will be found in these chapters. This book will lead you every step of the way.

Will there be a lot of work? Will you need to hustle? Take a guess.

Assignment: From Three Ideas To One
Idea #1

Filter 1: Briefly describe the Problem / Solution

Problem:

Solution:

Filter 2: Your Product / Service

Describe what it is and why it is a good solution to the problem:

Filter 3: The Customer

Demographics: Age, Sex, Income, Education etc.

Psychographics: Environmentally conscious? Active lifestyle? Socially focused? Tech Savvy? Image Conscious? Financially focused?

Filter 4: The Competition

Who are the competitors?

What is your differentiation?

Can you develop a niche?

Filter 5: The Business Model

Selling Price:

Cost:

Sales in Year 1:

When will you be profitable:

Money required to start up:

Strength of Idea

On a scale of 1 (poor) to 10 (home run!), what is the rating for this idea:

Idea #2

Filter 1: Briefly describe the Problem / Solution

Problem:

Solution:

Filter 2: Your Product / Service

Describe what it is and why it is a good solution to the problem:

Filter 3: The Customer

Demographics: Age, Sex, Income, Education etc.

Psychographics: Environmentally conscious? Active lifestyle? Socially focused? Tech Savvy? Image Conscious? Financially focused?

Filter 4: The Competition

Who are the competitors?

What is your differentiation?

Can you develop a niche?

Filter 5: The Business Model

Selling Price:

Cost:

Sales in Year 1:

When will you be profitable:

Money required to start up:

Strength of Idea

On a scale of 1 (poor) to 10 (home run!), what is the rating for this idea:

Idea #3

Filter 1: Briefly describe the Problem / Solution

Problem:

Solution:

Filter 2: Your Product / Service

Describe what it is and why it is a good solution to the problem:

Filter 3: The Customer

Demographics: Age, Sex, Income, Education etc.

Psychographics: Environmentally conscious? Active lifestyle? Socially focused? Tech Savvy? Image Conscious? Financially focused?

Filter 4: The Competition

Who are the competitors?

What is your differentiation?

Can you develop a niche?

Filter 5: The Business Model

Selling Price:

Cost:

Sales in Year 1:

When will you be profitable:

Money required to start up:

Strength of Idea

On a scale of 1 (poor) to 10 (home run!), what is the rating for this idea:

Picking One Idea

It's time to pick one idea. The above filter approach may have already given you a clear winner. Here are some additional guidelines we offer:

Factors that favor an idea (note that you don't have to have them all)
- o   You and your team are all passionate about it.
- o   It's a hobby for at least one member of the team.
- o   You or a team member is in the target market of customers.
- o   The product or service has a reasonable price point and will be easy and inexpensive to test out.
- o   There is not a lot of direct competition.
- o   Your business model is one that will allow you to make money.

Factors that don't favor an idea
- o   Lack of interest and passion.
- o   The idea is too complex.
- o   You're not sure who your target market is, or they can't afford or access your product.
- o   It requires technology that doesn't exist (unless the idea is new technology).

Your Starting Idea:

What idea would you like to pursue?

Why did you pick that one?

Write a brief synopsis of why your idea will succeed:

Take a deep breath. CELEBRATE. You've passed an important milestone. You have taken the first step.

Additional Notes

Chapter 3

SKILLS NEEDED
FOR ENTREPRENEURSHIP

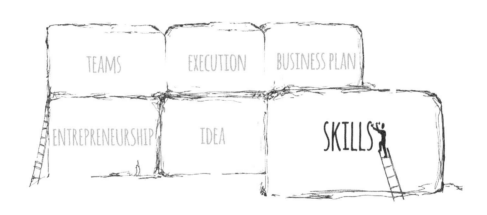

"He who knows others is wise; he who knows himself is enlightened." - Lao Tzu

"Great leaders know they can accomplish more by concentrating on their strengths—rather than always correcting their weakness." - Lolly Daskai

"There is no 'i' in team but there is in win." - Michael Jordan

~~~~~~~~

Key Topics in this Chapter

- Skills needed for entrepreneurship

- Self-Assessment: What skills do I have?

- How will I assemble the skills that I do not have?

- Team Strengths

- Assignment: Developing Your Team

"What are the skills needed for entrepreneurship? Which of these skills do I have? How do I even know what skills I have? Where will all the needed skills come from?" These maybe questions racing through your mind.

In this chapter we will try and answer most of these questions. Let's start by looking at what it takes to succeed in being an entrepreneur. Perhaps you will breathe a sigh of relief when you realize that you do not need to be a Wonder Woman or Superman, just a hardworking, committed and disciplined mortal.

Skills Needed for Entrepreneurship

One of the assignments that my students are asked to complete is: *"What does it take to be a successful entrepreneur? Do you have this or not? Elaborate."* As you can imagine, the answers are provocative, insightful and always revealing. One of the papers I remember vividly is that of a student taking me breathlessly on a roller coaster ride. He told me all the skills that were needed, all the things he did not like and probably could not do, but ended with a flourish exclaiming that he could not imagine working for others all his life. Therefore, he had no choice but to become an entrepreneur. Self-discovery is part of this journey.

The most common skills that the students come up with are: passion, integrity, persistence, resilience, endurance, hard work, resourcefulness, drive, discipline, vision, initiative, innovation, problem solving, curiosity, leadership, teamwork, self-awareness and strong network.

This is by no means an exhaustive list. Also, many of these themes are overlapping (e.g. persistence, resilience and endurance). In fact, all these skills are desirable. What if you could choose only five key skills, what would they be? What would these *Fundamental Skills* be?

Here is my list:

1. *Passion:* You must believe in your idea. You must live it, dream it and breathe it. Others will feed off your passion. Passion will also *get you through the inevitable trying moments.*

2. *Problem Solving:* It seems to me that almost everything about entrepreneurship relates to solving problems. Your business idea must solve a problem. You will undoubtedly confront many roadblocks and problems that you will need to resolve and overcome.

3. *Persistence:* Doing your own thing is not easy. There will be challenges and a certain "stick-to-itiveness" is essential - "grit" if you will. You have to get through the setbacks that accompany any great endeavor. Resilience, resourcefulness and endurance all seem to fall under this category.

4. *Execution:* Most enterprises and people, talk and plan a lot, but end up doing very little. Without execution, even the greatest of ideas is a waste. Simply put, you must have the capacity to get things done.

5. *Emotional Intelligence:* You will have to deal with and understand a variety of people, build a team and convince investors, suppliers and customers. IQ and hard work can only get you so far. It is connecting with people – emotional intelligence – that will propel you to much greater success. Leadership, powered by emotional intelligence, will take you much further than being a charismatic spellbinder who cannot relate to individuals.

Integrity has not been listed as a factor because *it is a given.* You must approach everything with integrity. It must be the hallmark of who you are, how you choose to live your life and what you stand for. Why would you ever compromise this? If you are still wondering if this is a good philosophy, ask yourself what kind of partners would you like: Those with integrity or those who are likely to cheat you?

In addition to these fundamental characteristics, there are certain other specific skills - let's call them functional skills - that will be needed by the enterprise.

Functional Skills

What might some of these be? If you are working on an app, you will need coding skills. Other skills that may be required could include website development, marketing, selling, research, creativity, making mock ups and developing financial projections. The list is likely to be long. Perhaps some of this can be outsourced, but that costs money and your budget may limit this option.

At this juncture you have probably hit the panic button. You don't have all the skills that are needed. *What are you going to do?*

Relax. No one person embodies all these skills. Let's first ask ourselves: "What skills do I have?" Then you can move on to addressing the next question: "How will I assemble the skills that I do not have?"

Does this sound like a plan? Let's keep going.

Self-Assessment: What Skills Do I Have?

Since time immemorial, the sages have urged us to: *Know thyself.* While they did not specifically have entrepreneurship in mind, their advice is useful for what you are trying to do.

I would like you to do the same assignment as my students: *"What skills does it take to be a successful entrepreneur? Do you have these skills or not? Elaborate."*

My students use four pages, which allow for reasonable depth. I suggest you do the same. You will learn a fair bit about your strengths, fears and the inherent possibilities that surround you.

After completing the above assignment, make an inventory of the following:

- My Five Top Skills Are:
- I Am Most Scared Of:
- Functional Skills: I am good at:
- For my (our) Business Idea, the Most Critical Skills we will need are:

To do this exploration at a deeper level, involve a few of your close friends, family members and colleagues. Ask them what they think are your top five skills. Often others see us far more clearly than we see ourselves. As scary as this may sound, the learning will be invaluable.

Using *StrengthsFinder* To Find Your Five Top Skills

You may have taken the Myers-Briggs test. It is a helpful indicator of who you are and how you approach things. A few years back I took the *StrengthsFinder* quiz and was quite surprised by what I learned about myself. I then convinced some of my family members to do the same and it was fascinating what we learned about each other. I now recommend this exercise to my students. Recently, my banker told me he was getting married and I recommended that he and his fiancée do this exercise as it would help them understand each other better.

What exactly is this test? The Gallup organization has developed a database of several million successful people and the skills they possess. They have identified 34 key skills, as shown in the chart below, grouped into four categories: Executing, Relationship, Influence, and Strategic.

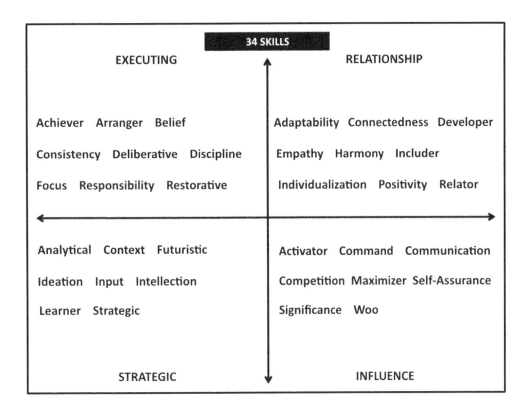

However, here is the real important insight. While all of us have many of these skills, *we should focus on our top skills.* Why? Because it has been said, *"We achieve exceptional things leveraging our strengths, not working on our weaknesses."* This is a huge insight and contrary to what we have been taught all our lives.

Author Marcus Buckingham explains it this way: *"Parents dwell on a child's 'F' in Algebra rather than praise an 'A' in English. In a one-hour performance review, supervisors spend two minutes discussing strengths and 58 minutes discussing the 'areas of opportunity' or weaknesses with employees...."*

This statement hit particularly close to home since this is what we did with our children. We thought that they had to excel in everything. We took the 'A's in English for granted while lamenting the lower grades in Math. As I reflect, all the extra time spent on math yielded little fruit. What if all that time had been spent cultivating exceptionalism in English?

This is the premise of StrengthsFinder. By answering about 180 questions in 30 minutes, you will be presented with your *Top 5 Strengths*. The reality is that while we have many strengths, we are genetically coded for a handful of things. By focusing on these strengths, you will achieve more than trying to cover the entire waterfront. (For example, if you are not very good at learning foreign languages, spending a lifetime trying to learn French will, at most, make you a passably poor speaker. What if you spent the same time working on something you are good at? How did Michael Jordan do when he tried his hand at baseball?)

So take this test (gallupstrengthscenter.com/Purchase). It may be the best $20 you ever spend.

Shortly after you take the quiz (sounds better than a test), you will receive a 20-page document giving you details about your five top strengths. You will be surprised by how well they understand you. I know I was. This is an important piece of the jigsaw puzzle labeled *"You."*

Let's take a look at an actual example. A person, whom we will call Mike, took this survey and the results indicated that his top 5 strengths are: *Focus, Achiever, Learner, Self-Assurance and Relator.*

The report from StrengthsFinder will give you one-page detailed descriptions for each of these themes. To give you a quick sense of how it looks, below is a brief summary of Mike's strengths that we have paraphrased from the above report.

- *Focus*: You ask yourself everyday, "Where am I headed?" and strive to move towards your goal. You do not allow the team to wander.

- *Achiever*: Great deal of stamina and works hard. Quite open with individuals or groups. The trust you have for a person dictates how much you reveal.

- *Strategic*: Innovative, inventive, original and resourceful. You venture beyond the commonplace, familiar, or obvious.

- *Self-Assurance*: Have faith in your strengths, abilities and judgment. Always seem to know the right decisions; not easily swayed by other's opinions.

- *Relator*: Enjoy close relationships. Selective with relationships; would rather deepen your existing relationships than create superficial new ones.

We take this data and develop this pictorial.

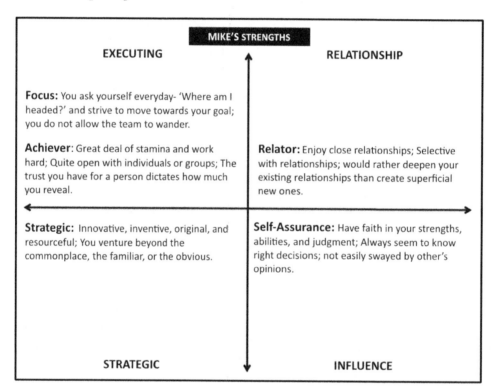

When you get your results, embrace your five skills. Leverage your genetically coded abilities to excel at whatever you choose to do.

With all the work you have done you will have a better idea of *"Who am I? What are my strengths? What was I born to do?"* Well done! You are learning to dig deeper and that too is a part of the entrepreneurial mindset. The other thought that you are likely to have is: *"I cannot possibly do this start up alone!"*

How will I assemble the skills that I do not have?

The answer is clear: Entrepreneurship is best done as a team!

Perhaps you already have partners. Great. Maybe you have some people in mind. Good. (If you truly want to work alone, these other skills can be outsourced. But outsourced vendors are unlikely to have the passion and desire that a start-up will need.)

What if you do not have partners but would like to find some. What should you look for?

These are some things we suggest you consider:

- *Commonalities of Values:* This is crucial. You must have common values. Without such commonalities, life will be a struggle.
- *Diversity of Experiences:* Such differences will allow you to look at the world with different perspectives, thereby letting you find many different ways to solve problems.
- *Diversity of Thought:* This is crucial. You do not want "Yes" people. You want people who are independent thinkers, people who may think very differently from you yet have the courage to voice that opinion. In that distinction lies a sea of creativity.
- *Different skill sets:* If the other person is just like you, one of you is redundant, most likely *you*.
- *Team Players:* Prima Donnas, as smart or talented as they may be, are never worth it. Being a team player means working towards team goals. Personal agendas are a distraction.
- *Shared Goals:* Do you want to go the same place, in the same way?

It is better to get to know the team members before they become team members. A bit of work ahead of time may be one of the best investments that you make. It will save you the trouble and time of training someone who is not a right fit.

How do you do this? Ask for references; and then speak to these references. Spend 30 minutes asking questions about a person. Ask three or four references the same questions and you will develop a pretty good idea about the person. Their social media pages may also hold useful insights. Ask them to come to work with you for 90 days before making any firm commitments. Cut your losses quickly. Cherish the good ones.

When I think about the teams that have done well, it seems that they have a common passion. They develop an ability to "call each other out." Often they will go through a crisis. Perhaps an idea crashes and burns, one person is not carrying his fair share of the load, or someone is sucking up the oxygen. The first instinct of a team is to let things slide. Invariably the work suffers and the team is miserable. Finally, a confrontation will occur. Harsh words may be exchanged and even some tears shed, but the whole experience will be cathartic. I have seen teams doing a barely adequate job suddenly swing into high gear and deliver great results. Surviving the crucible leads to smiles, a deeper sense of teamwork and the dawning belief that success is within reach.

Team Strengths

I suggest that you have everyone take the StrengthsFinder survey. Then take the results and plot it like you see here. Be prepared to be amazed at what you learn.

I have taken four people (whose names have been changed) who worked on a team and plotted their data, first individually and then as a team. Besides Mike, we have Sophia, Jim and Emily. Take a few minutes to see every person's strengths and then see how all the strengths add up.

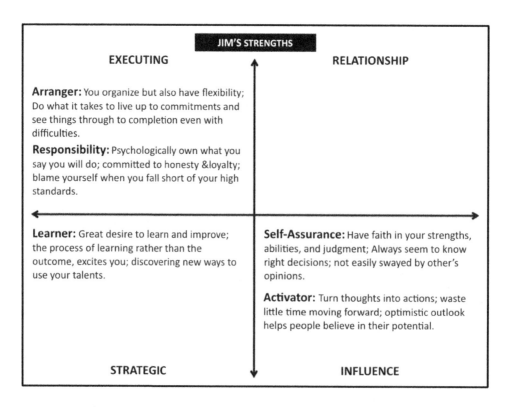

SOPHIA'S STRENGTHS

EXECUTING

RELATIONSHIP

Responsibility: Psychologically own what you say you will do; committed to honesty &loyalty; blame yourself when you fall short of your high standards.

Achiever: Great deal of stamina and work hard; Quite open with individuals or groups; The trust you have for a person dictates how much you reveal.

Arranger: You organize but also have flexibility; Do what it takes to live up to commitments and see things through to completion even with difficulties.

Individualization: Don't like generalizations; everyone is different; Recognize people's unique qualities and strengths; Good at building teams.

Activator: Turn thoughts into actions; waste little time moving forward; optimistic outlook helps people believe in their potential.

STRATEGIC

INFLUENCE

JIM'S STRENGTHS

EXECUTING

RELATIONSHIP

Arranger: You organize but also have flexibility; Do what it takes to live up to commitments and see things through to completion even with difficulties.

Responsibility: Psychologically own what you say you will do; committed to honesty &loyalty; blame yourself when you fall short of your high standards.

Learner: Great desire to learn and improve; the process of learning rather than the outcome, excites you; discovering new ways to use your talents.

Self-Assurance: Have faith in your strengths, abilities, and judgment; Always seem to know right decisions; not easily swayed by other's opinions.

Activator: Turn thoughts into actions; waste little time moving forward; optimistic outlook helps people believe in their potential.

STRATEGIC

INFLUENCE

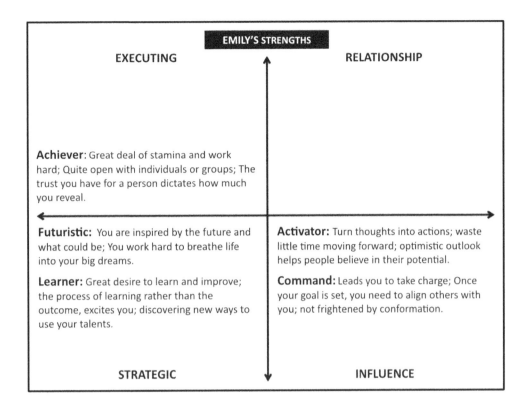

It looks like the team members have different strengths. **What does the team look like as a unit?** For that, let's combine these results.

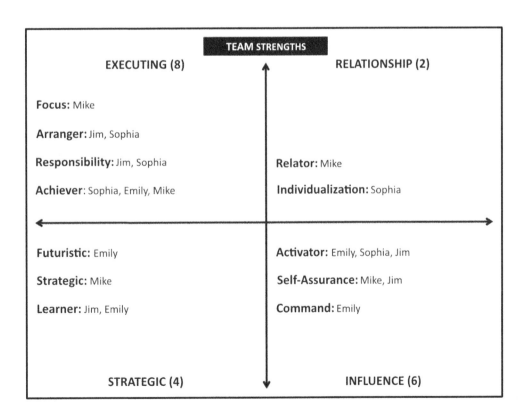

What thoughts come to your mind as you look at the combined skills of the team? Here is what I deduce:

- The team has strengths in all quadrants. Whew! That's a relief.
- Four team members with five strengths each, means that the team has a total of 20 Key Strengths chips. How are these distributed?
- The Executing skill is strong. Good, it means things will get done.
- Strategy and Influence have good representation.
- On the relationship side, the team is a bit low. It does *not* mean that the team members do not care about relationships. It does mean that the team is naturally more inclined to focus on the other elements. By becoming aware of this, you can make an extra effort to focus more on both internal and external relationships.
- This chart can also help you figure out the best way to communicate with each other. By making it a point to understand each other better, you will develop much stronger Relationships.

A few final thoughts about StrengthsFinder: The data is directional, not absolute. Remember that each of us has more than just the five skills, but it is those five skills that we are strongest at.

In this chapter you have explored your own skills and learned about the skills of your teammates. You now have a sense of what is required to succeed and how you might go about doing so. Teams can help make the entrepreneurial journey more fun, productive and successful.

"You get the best out of others when you give the best of yourself." - Harvey Firestone

"If you can't feed a team with two pizzas, it's too large." - Jeff Bezos, Amazon

It is time to get started on building a great team and time to start the next chapter!

Assignment: Developing Your Team

Start by doing an assessment of the skills that you and the team have as well as the skills the business will need. The list is long. You are not likely to have all the skills needed. No need to panic. That's where team members and outsourcing come in.

Entrepreneurship Skill Assessment Chart: On a scale of 1-10, 1=Lousy, 10=Exceptional, rate yourself and your teammates. (A four-person team has been assumed; adjust as needed).

	Fundamental Skills	**#1**	**#2**	**#3**	**#4**
1	**Integrity**				
2	Passion				
3	Problem Solving				
4	Persistence				
5	Execution				
6	Emotional Intelligence				
	Other Desirable Skills				
1	Willing to work hard and long hours				
2	Family / Social support to strike off on my own				
3	Comfortable with the instability that may come				
4	Can function in ambiguous situation				
5	Good network of friends and business acquaintances				
6	Get along with a variety of different types of people				
7	Have a high *sustainable* energy level				
8	Good understanding of how to manage a business				
9	Believe that I am primarily responsible for my own successes and failures				
	Functional Skills that Will Be Needed				
1					
2					
3					
4					
5					

After each member of the team has taken the StrengthsFinder quiz, plot your team's results below.

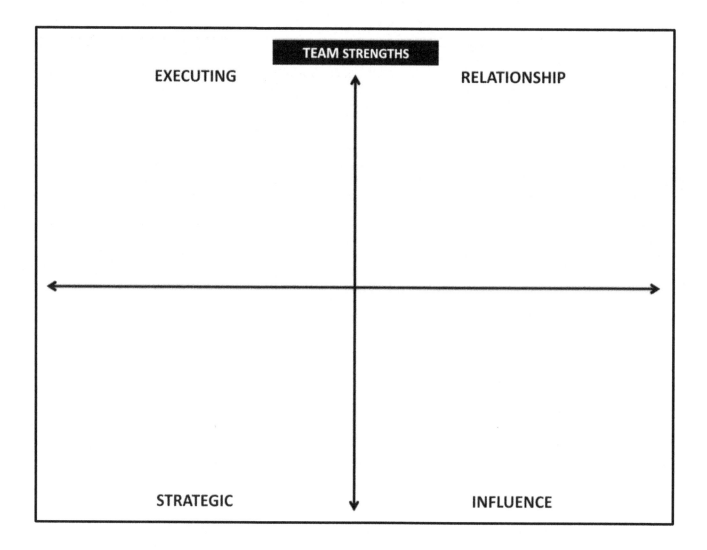

How does your team look? Do you have a balance of skills? Are you ready to leverage your strengths?

Additional Notes

Chapter 4

BUILDING A TEAM

"Teamwork is the ability to work together toward a common vision. The ability to direct individual accomplishments toward organizational objectives. It is the fuel that allows common people to attain uncommon results." - Andrew Carnegie

"The strength of the team is each individual member. The strength of each member is the team." - Phil Jackson

"Happy families are all alike; every unhappy family is unhappy in its own way." - Leo Tolstoy in Anna Karenina

~~~~~~~~

Key Topics in this Chapter

- Team Experiences

- Dysfunctionality

- Engendering Trust

- What Do Good Teams Look Like?

- A Circuit Breaker

- Team Charter

- Some Thoughts On People

- Assignment: Develop Your Team Charter and Assessments

Team Experiences

How many teams have you been a part of? Think of all the sports you've played, the theater ensembles you've acted in, fund raising drives you've participated in, or perhaps the businesses you have worked in. I imagine it adds up to quite a few teams.

How many of those teams did you have fun with? Did you enjoy the people and the work, feel involved and productive? Did the team succeed?

Now reflect on the teams where you did not have fun, where people constantly bickered, not much was achieved and you could not wait for the misery to end.

An unpleasant team experience is not uncommon. Do some of these memories resonate?

- The goal was never clear.
- No one really knew who was supposed to do what.
- The timeline was never laid out.
- People seemed to have their own agendas.
- Nobody seemed to listen to each other.
- People often clashed.
- Cliques formed.
- Meetings were long, unfocused and unsatisfactory.
- There seemed to be a need to blame someone.
- Commitments were made but no one was held accountable.
- The focus was on "I" and not "We."

Was any of this fun or productive? *If you want to achieve different results, you must take a different path.*

Dysfunctionality

Dysfunctional teams are the norm. A key reason is *structure*. Often teams do not clearly understand the desired outcome. Who is responsible for doing what, by when? What are the ground rules for behavior?

Perhaps the most fundamental requirement that human beings have for working with each other is "trust." There is something in our human psyche that requires *trust* in order to develop a deep, satisfying and productive relationship. Steven Covey puts it thus:

> *"Trust is the glue of life. It's the most essential ingredient in effective communication. It's the foundational principle that holds all relationships."*

Now reflect on all your experiences and ask yourself how often did you truly trust your teammates?

Some years back I was at a dinner in Washington, DC, and found myself sitting next to a young man, a colonel, who had just come back from a tour of duty in Iraq. We started to discuss leadership and teams. He shared with me how he and his team had developed great trust by getting to know each other and really listening to each other. Such trust is paramount where decisions can mean the difference between life and death. Over time, the trust became second nature and they learned to listen to each other without thinking twice. One time he was about to knock on a door when one of his men shouted "duck." Without knowing why, or thinking twice, he dropped to the ground instantaneously, thereby avoiding an exploding door that had been booby-trapped. He felt he knew his men's likes and dislikes deeply and understood them as well as he did his own wife. Every team member felt this way.

It is true that war demands a certain closeness, intensity and belief. However, in a way, so does the birth of a new company. The people are few and they must depend on each other to an enormous degree. Starting a company is a close second, outside of war, to getting married. Finding the right partner(s) is crucial.

Patrick Lencioni[8] in his book *Five Dysfunctions of a Team* looks at team dynamics and their inherent dysfunction thoughtfully and engagingly. I also suggest looking at his website (tablegroup.com). Let's take a look at these five dysfunctions.

1. **Absence of Trust:** The sad reality is that people do not trust each other easily. It is common to hide behind a façade. Facebook may be the ultimate mask that one puts on. What is real, what is true, who are we really? Who knows? We do not want to be vulnerable, so we hide and we pretend to be invulnerable. What are we so afraid of? Back to our old friend - *fear*. Fear of being hurt. Fear of being let down. Fear of not being good enough… you know the story.

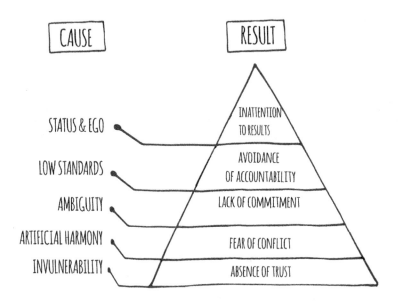

2. **Fear of Conflict:** When there is no trust, people avoid any conflict of ideas, leading to artificial harmony. They don't really believe in what is being said, or advocated, but it is too much trouble challenging other people. Besides, if you challenge someone, you might be challenged back. Who needs that, right? It's much better to nod your head, smile and get the meeting over with as quickly as possible so you can get back to all that work piling up on your desk. Sound familiar?

3. **Lack of Commitment:** As you walk out of the meeting, commitment to the goals is the last thing on your mind. The phone calls you have to return are far more pressing. You feel that most of the goals are crazy and unachievable and in any case, Tom (or X, Y, or Z) never follows up. How could you really commit to these so-called team goals? From my days of working in a big company, I still can recall many times when business leaders made implausible commitments to deliver heroic results. This would be followed a few months later with a new story and a new reason for the lack of results. Companies create cultures by their actions. This organization had inadvertently created a culture of earnest oratory and flashy presentations, with little emphasis on true commitment and accountability.

---

[8] Lencioni, Patrick. *Five Dysfunctions of a Team*. San Francisco: Jossey –Bass, 2002.

4. **Avoidance of Accountability:** Not surprisingly there is not much accountability in such organizations. Excuses readily sprout up. Blame, if needed, is quickly apportioned to some unlucky soul with less political skills. It's all a game.

5. **Poor Results:** The results are usually disappointing. People take credit for what little has gone right and then pin the failures elsewhere. It is said that success has a thousand fathers, but failure is an orphan. Poor results, before we know it, become the norm.

I have come to realize that exceptional teams are the exception. In most organizations, the overwhelming force of inertia makes change very hard. Change implies something different, something that may fail. Better to stay with the known mediocrity than venture into a new land of unknown possibilities. I have seen companies getting destroyed because people remained tied to their own personal interests rather than work as a team. Sometimes organizations will start on the path of change, but declare a premature victory and stop after a small amount of progress has been made.

This is both depressing and commonplace as attested to by this 2013 *Forbes* article headline: *"Unhappy Employees Outnumber Happy Ones By Two To One Worldwide."* Very simply, unhappy employees mean unhappy dysfunctional teams. How then will you do things differently? How will you create a culture of trust, accountability and results?

Engendering Trust

What is required to build trust? Perhaps Emerson had the answer: *"Trust men and they will be true to you; treat them greatly and they will show themselves great."*

The starting point of trust is getting to know each other. You need to be willing to be vulnerable, share your fears, weaknesses and to listen with an open mind. How do we do this? By spending time together, sharing and listening. Let me tell you about *three exercises*, among many, that I have used. None of which, by the way, were created by me:

The first exercise is called *Six Questions* where each team member takes 10 minutes to answer these questions:

1. Where were you born?
2. How many siblings did you have?
3. What was the most challenging experience you had growing up?
4. What was the best job you ever had and why?
5. What was the worst job you ever had and why?
6. Share something that very few people know about you.

You will be surprised as to how much you can learn about a person by just listening to their answers. Human beings have a need to share and open up, but this can only be achieved in an atmosphere of trust.

The second exercise is called *Share Your Shield*. The various segments of the shield are designed for the participants to share their inner feelings. How do you see yourself? How do you think people see you?

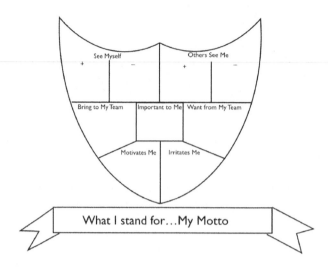

What can you offer others and what would you like others to help you with? What motivates you and what irritates you?

The mottos - what people stand for - are always interesting and revealing.

Give everyone about 20 minutes to complete this exercise. Then take 10 minutes to share what they have written. Listen attentively. Ask only clarifying questions; do not make editorial comments.

Being vulnerable is not easy. Create the environment that allows people to open up and share their dreams, hopes, fears, limitations and aspirations. Most people do this exercise and move on. I suggest you keep everyone's "shields," as well as your own and periodically look at them. There is much learning and desire, embedded in them.

The third exercise, called the *Johari Window,* is especially helpful when the team has worked together for a few months. It focuses on the "Blind Self," a side of ourselves that we do not see but others do. The purpose of this exercise is for our teammates to help us see this hidden part.

1. Known Self	2. Hidden Self
Things we know about ourselves and others know about us	Things we know about ourselves and others know about us
3. Blind Self	4. Unknown Self
Things others know about us that we do not know	Things neither we nor others know about us

Everyone jots down two things about the other people in the room: 1) Things they do that are positive and helpful to the team and 2) Things that they do, perhaps inadvertently, which hurt the team.

The team starts with giving feedback to one person, generally the leader. One at a time, you tell this person what you see their positive attributes to be. The recipient of these comments can only ask a clarifying question but cannot defend, make any other comments, or argue. At the end of the positive feedback, this person will say, "Thank you." That's it. Now the team shares the second part of the equation: things that you would like this person to improve or abstain from. The same norms apply: no arguments, just a simple, "Thank you." The recipient is advised to write down all feedback.

Go clockwise, giving feedback to one member at a time. The results are generally received very well. The positive feedback touches people and I see them genuinely moved. The constructive feedback is also received with respect. A few months later when I check in with people as to how they are doing, they have invariably worked to diminish, or stop, their undesirable behavior.

There are many such exercises. Please keep using them and getting to know each other better. Truly understanding someone takes time. Be respectful of the other person's feelings. However, you must also be honest. Being politically correct is both demeaning and unproductive. The purpose is to give constructive feedback and help one another grow. In an atmosphere of trust, virtually all things can be put on the table and addressed.

Everything starts with *trust*.

What Do Good Teams Look Like?

With this sturdy foundation of trust, it is now time to address the other dysfunctions.

The fake harmony should be discarded. Very simply, conflict of ideas is healthy, but a conflict of personalities is cancerous. Argue about the ideas as much as you like, but don't demonize one another or someone's point of view. The permission to do this comes from the trust you have built.

Since everyone has had a say and has been listened to, *commitment* comes more easily. People do not demand that their point of view be accepted, but they do want to be heard. Whenever people feel they have had an input into something, they feel committed to it. The outcome becomes "ours."

With these steps, people embrace personal accountability. Even more importantly, they hold their teammates accountable for the goals that were assigned to them. Everything then is about team goals and not about *me*, what I did and what others did not do. Remember people *do* like to accomplish things and *do* like to be held accountable as long as *everyone* is being held accountable.

Not surprisingly results improve. While good results can never be guaranteed, the likelihood of better results is enhanced. More importantly, the journey becomes fun.

My good friend, Professor Adam Goodman, Director of The Center for Leadership at Northwestern University, makes several suggestions to my students as they embark on forming teams.

- Get to know each other by spending time together.
- Talk in person whenever possible as opposed to emailing and texting.
- Come to the team meetings on time.
- Come prepared having done all the homework you were supposed to do.
- Come ready with your questions and suggestions.
- Learn to have honest conversations, not polite ones.
- Clearly define the tasks and roles for each member.
- Demonstrate your commitment through small wins as opposed to trying to impress people with big things.

Does anything seem like brain surgery here? No. It is simple. It is a lot of singles and very few, if any, home runs. But why is it so hard then? The reasons lie in our impatience, which has been made worse by the onslaught of the 24/7 tools of technology. Slow down, breathe and finish what you have committed to doing, now.

Professor Goodman further counsels: speak less, listen more, ask questions, talk about mistakes and seek feedback. Understand differing perspectives, pick what is best for the team and self-reflect often. Embedded in this advice is a lifetime of wisdom.

Building a team is akin to cultivating a garden. It takes time, energy, water and a big dollop of nourishing. Every human being is both similar and different. We need to work with both ends of this spectrum to discover and unleash the richness that lies within.

Before asking others to do something, I have often found it better to set the example myself. *A leader does not do what he wants to do; he does what is required to be done.* I once witnessed a team that was in total disarray come together quickly, productively and joyously, when the leader took the feedback to heart and changed the way she approached the team. Are you a leader? If so, you must lead the change.

A Circuit Breaker

Will your team break down at some point? You can bet on it. Someone will develop a penchant for being late or always have an excuse for not getting their assignment done. Another person may suck up all the oxygen in a room while the "quiet" one will rarely participate because "he prefers to listen."

Sometimes you will need to talk to a person alone and other times it's best to do it as a team. The circumstances will dictate which route you take. In either case, consider following these words of wisdom from John Maxwell, who writes and speaks on leadership:

> - Do it as soon as possible after the incident.
> - Speak to one issue at a time.
> - Don't keep repeating the same thing. Do it once.
> - Avoid sarcasm.
> - Avoid words like "never" and "always."
> - Present criticism as suggestions.
> - Don't apologize for the confrontational meeting.
> - Don't forget the compliments.

Once again, these are all basic courtesies that we should readily afford one another. However, in our emotional state, we are prone to forget. Have I ever repeated myself? Been sarcastic? Dredged up three lifetimes of history? Did I ever win the argument? Surely you jest.

A student shared this story: "We had been doing great work throughout the quarter, but one of our team members was constantly late. It was starting to grate on us as we felt that his lateness indicated a lack of dedication to the team and that it was hurting our efficiency. We sat down, shared our feelings and told him that we wanted everyone to do the best work possible. We were open and honest and so was he and things improved greatly from thereon."

So, do not be afraid to use this circuit breaker when needed. You will be far more effective and less stressed.

A Team Contract

A few years ago, I used Professor Goodman's methodology and starting asking my students to develop a team contract at the outset. The teamwork has improved considerably.

Here is another anecdote from a student: "There was something about having the structure of the charter in the very beginning. We took the time to sit down together in my living room and seriously thought about what we individually wanted to get and give in the class, but more importantly, what we as a team wanted to achieve. Getting down on paper what we'd need to do to be successful solidified our sense of camaraderie and got us excited for the endless possibilities the future held."

I recommend you develop a team contract too. RIGHT NOW! Here is how to do it:

To Do as Individuals
- Think about a team that you were on that was highly successful. Write down three factors that you think made that happen.

- o Think about a team that you were on, that was a failure and a miserable experience for you. Write down three factors that you think made that happen.
- o What lessons did you learn from the above?

To Do as a Team
- o Discuss lessons learned above.
- o What things are important to the team members and the project?
- o Develop a team Charter with the following components:
    - Lay out some things you will do and will not do.
    - What behaviors are desirable and what are not?
    - How will you treat each other?
    - How will you listen to each other?
    - We suggest no more than *five* guiding behaviors.

Revisit the charter every month to discuss how your team is doing. Revise as necessary.

Some Thoughts on People

In reading the works of Jim Collins, Peter Drucker, John Maxwell and others, as well as thinking of my own experiences, I have been struck by how important it is to have the right people in the organization. Jim Collins' notion of *"First Who, Then What"* reiterates the fact that people are more important than ideas. The right people are not motivated by money. Yes, of course they need to make a living, but they are motivated by something far greater, namely learning, growing and making the organization successful and exceptional. Such people always do the right thing. They like to be trusted, given responsibility and they deliver exceptional results. They hold themselves responsible to a standard much higher than anything you can possibly ask for.

When you find such people, hang on to them. They don't come often. Work to find the right seat for them. What should you do if you are not sure of someone? Take a pass. Wait until you find the right person. Character is the most important trait that I want in a team member. Nowadays most skills can be outsourced, but not character and integrity.

If perchance you happen to get a person who does not have character on your team, hope like heck, as Warren Buffett said, that they are stupid, because otherwise the consequences will be disastrous.

"Most people say that it is the intellect which makes a great scientist. They are wrong: it is character." - Albert Einstein

"People grow through experience if they meet life honestly and courageously. This is how character is built." - Eleanor Roosevelt

"Be more concerned with your character than your reputation, because your character is what you really are, while your reputation is merely what others think you are." - John Wooden

ASSIGNMENTS: Team Contract, Assessment and More

Team Contract
1.
2.
3.
4.
5.

Your Team Assessment: On a scale of 1-10, 1=Lousy, 10=Exceptional, each member of your team should give a rating for each of the five factors.

	Five Dysfunctions	#1	#2	#3	#4
1	Absence of Trust				
2	Fear of Conflict				
3	Lack of Commitment				
4	Avoidance of Accountability				
5	Poor Results				
	Average				
	Range				

There should be no finger pointing. Listen to each other. *Everything starts with Trust.* Keep working on building trust. Do this exercise every quarter.

Engendering Trust

Month 1: Do the "Six Questions" exercise

Date Completed: _____

Month 3: Do the "Share Your Shield" exercise

Date Completed: _____

Month 6: Do the "Johari Window" exercise

Date Completed: _____

Every quarter do a new team exercise. You can find plenty of them on the web. The key is to get to know each other better. You will benefit; the team will benefit.

Quarterly Assessment

On a scale of 1-10, 1=Lousy, 10=Exceptional, each member of the team should rate how good the team is today.

Average Rating: _____   Range: _____

Discuss. Are you following the team contract? Does it need to be revised?

Additional Notes

Chapter 5

EXECUTION

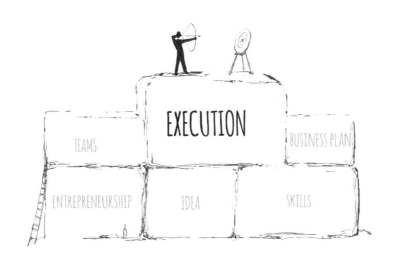

"Vision without action is a daydream. Action without vision is a nightmare." - Japanese Proverb

"This is so simple it sounds stupid, but it is amazing how few oil people really understand that you only find oil if you drill wells. You may think you're finding it when you're drawing maps and studying logs, but you have to drill." - John Masters in The Hunters

"To me, ideas are worth nothing unless executed.
They are just a multiplier. Execution is worth millions." - Steve Jobs

~~~~~~~~

Key Topics in this Chapter

- Getting Things Done Is Hard

- The Vision – VET (Vision & Execution Tracker) Page 1

- Execution – VET Page 2

- Weekly Meeting & Issues Resolution

- Assignment: Develop Your Team's VET

Getting Things Done is Hard

Dreaming is fun. Talking is easy. However, getting things done is really hard.

Most organizations develop detailed and lengthy plans. There is a minor problem though: most plans never come to fruition. Just look around you. Virtually all organizations talk about what they plan to do in lofty terms, mistaking their verbosity for actual results. *Size is a natural enemy of getting things done.* Governments and large organizations are a good example of this phenomenon. Numerous layers of management lead to greater bureaucracy, lengthy processes, less accountability, all of which then result in lesser productivity.

Size can be an inhibitor, but so can one's actions. How would you rate yourself? Do you regularly make deadlines? Did you finish that project you committed to? Is your inbox cleared out? Have you called your parents recently?

Entrepreneurs view themselves as people of ideas and action, and they are. But some of them also think of themselves as visionaries, dashing around, formulating ideas and directing action. Before anything is actually done, the word goes out - "Hold it"- the visionary has a new idea. While it can be exhilarating to play the lead role, chaos, bedlam, frustration, fear and ire are often the end result. An excerpt from a 2015 *Fortune* article titled *"Jawbone: The trials of a 16-year-old can't-miss startup,"* described the story of well-loved entrepreneurs with big ideas who often missed product deadlines. After 16 years they are still in the startup phase. Another article talks about "Fab the design-focused e-commerce site that said it would generate $250 million in revenue in 2013. It ended up bringing in around $100 million...Fab shrank from 750 employees to 150." Ideas and execution are different creatures.

Shakespeare[9] was evidently thinking about this when he developed the concept of *'Prattle without Practice"* in *Othello*. I have encountered many prattlers in my business life. Sometimes people prattle because they think their role as the head honcho demands it. Humans also babble when they are either bereft or have an overabundance of ideas. I plead guilty too. I love discussions and I take great pride in talking to the rank and file about all sorts of ideas. The problem is that when a boss utters an idea, it is sometimes hard to distinguish between an edict and an unformed suggestion that can be safely discarded. At the end of my first year of running a very large business, I was asked what the most important lesson I had learned was. "How to keep my mouth shut," was my answer.

How then do we move on from prattling to practice, ideation to getting things done and from dreaming to doing? The keys to execution are:

- Know what you want to achieve.
- Make someone responsible.
- Have this person define the task/project/action clearly.
- Set a clear achievable completion date.
- Monitor progress regularly and fix gaps if any.
- Hold the person accountable for delivering the results.

To capture these key elements, we have developed a two-page document we call *VET – Vision and Execution Tracker.* In doing so, we have been influenced by our own experiences, as well as the books of Gino Wickman[10] and Patrick Lencioni, among other authors. When we ask people whether bringing about such a level of clarity might lead to greater success, the answer is always a resounding "Yes!"

Capturing these key ideas and action steps is succinctly hard. We are reminded of this purported telegram exchange between Mark Twain and his publisher:

Publisher: *Need 2-page short story two days.*
Mark Twain: *No can do 2 pages two days. Can do 30 pages 2 days.*

---

[9] Shakespeare, William. *Othello*. UK: Thomas Walkley, 1622.

[10] Wickman, Gino. *Traction*. Dallas: BenBella Books, Inc., 2011

Need 30 days to do 2 pages.

Nevertheless, let us take on the challenge of developing such a two-pager. It seems that a similar process worked for John D. Rockefeller. I believe you can make it work for you too. The first page of the VET deals with the vision while the second page captures the execution that will be needed to deliver on this vision

The Vision

Vision deals with the long term. Depending on your business, this might be three, five, or ten years out. It captures your hopes, dreams and reason to be, along with some strategies and metrics. When done well, an employee, partner, banker, investor, or a supplier should be able to get a good idea of why you are in business, what you aspire to do and how you propose to get there. Not only does it try to define "there" but it also explains your operations. It is an ambitious goal to put this on one page but I have seen many companies, including some of my clients, do this quite successfully.

The work to get there is hard. The best results occur when a team - after discussion, disagreements and new insights - determines this vision. To make this "our" vision and "our" company, there must be the belief that "we" worked on it together. This requires that each member of the team feel he was listened to and the outcome was collaboratively arrived at. The Vision should be revisited, revised, or reaffirmed every year.

Let's examine the four major components of the Vision Tracker:

VET (Vision & Execution Tracker
Organization Name:

<u>Vision</u>: VET – Page 1

Purpose		Long Term Picture (3, 5, or 10 years)
Values		**Future Date:**
		<u>**Key Measurables (fit to your needs)**</u> 1. 2. 3. 4.
Five Filters		<u>**Key Challenges to make this happen**</u> 1. 2. 3. 4. 5.

66

Purpose: The purpose of a Vision is rarely about making money; it is tied to something far more compelling. It is emotional and it is a call to our greater self. What is our reason to be? What will make us wake up every morning excited and wanting to run to work? You need to capture this in a short pithy phrase.

Here is our best guess about the purposes of these companies:

- *Disney: To make people happy.*
- *Mary Kay: Empower Women.*
- *Southwest Airlines: Democratize air travel.*
- *Grameen Bank: Bank for the poor.*
- *Skype: To connect the world.*
- *Apple: To put a dent in the universe.*

Sometimes I see companies struggle with this, especially if they have been in existence for some time. Isn't it the purpose of a company to make money? What else is there? It is true that a business must make money to exist, but that is not the key reason for its existence. It has to be about alleviating a pain, bringing joy, empowering people and/or serving someone. Think of money as oxygen: a business needs it to survive. Now think of purpose as life. Oxygen allows you to live but it does not define or make your life.

Values: This may be the most important part of this exercise. What do you believe in? What do you stand for? What do you admire? What do you detest? How will you behave, with each other and with others? There may be a few basic values such as integrity and dependability. Most teams profess to have these but they may not be differentiating. What will make you unique? What behaviors will allow you to create something of great significance? Most organizations have these plastered all over the halls, but the more important question is: are any of them actually being practiced? There, alas, the story is not as cheerful. Therefore, we urge you to really think about what these values are. A good test is to determine whether the leadership team actually practices and embraces these values. (If not, they are not your current values. Perhaps they are aspirational. In any case, do not include any value that the leadership team is not practicing today.)

Below is an exercise we suggest for developing values:

1. Each member of the team, including you, should:
   a. Think of a person (from a past job experience or some aspect of your life) that you really would love to work with and have on the team. List three qualities of this person that make this person desirable as a teammate.
   b. Think of a person that you would absolutely NOT want on the team. List three qualities of such a person.
2. As a team, discuss these two sets of people.
3. Through that discussion, develop three to five values that you would want in every member of the company.
4. Now, it is time to ascertain whether the team members actually embody these values. To do that, you will need to develop a matrix like the one shown nearby.
   a. Use a check mark for a person who exhibits that quality
   b. Use an "X" for a person who does not exhibit that quality
   c. And use a "**?**" for a maybe.

VALUES EXERCISE

VALUES	Integrity	Optimistic	Team Player	Can-Do	Customer Focused
Mike	✔	✔	✔	✔	✘
Sophia	✔	?	✔	?	?
Jim	✔	?	✔	✘	?
Emily	✔	✔	✔	✔	✘

5. You will remember these team members from their appearance in a previous chapter. What does this chart tell you? The good news is that everyone has integrity and is a team player. But on "optimism," Sophia and Jim will need to do better. It is also clear that none of the team members are customer focused. That, then, is not a current value. The team may aspire to own this value someday, but it is not true today. So skip that value for now. There is also a problem with the "Can-Do" value. Specifically, Jim does not embody it. For that to be a team value, Jim has to change dramatically, or he has to leave the team, or you have to drop that value. For an aspirational value, start practicing that value first and only when it is embedded in your culture make it a company value.

Does this seem like a lot of work? Perhaps, but it might be the most important thing that you will do as a team. Teams are built on trust. This comes from belief, behavior and adherence to the values. *Less Prattle, More Practice* is the operating mantra here.

Five Filters: You remember these questions from an earlier chapter. As promised, no work goes to waste. Why do you want these in the Vision statement? They will remind you about the key underpinnings of your business. You would be surprised how often mission creep occurs and bored executives, aided by consultants and investment bankers, get attracted and distracted with shiny new things. Be wary of any distractions.

Develop one-sentence answers to each of the filters. This will keep you focused.

1. Problem - Solution?
2. What is your product?
3. Who is your customer?
4. Who is your competition?
5. What is your business model? Specifically, how will you make money?

Long Term Picture: Pick a future date; it can be three, five, or ten years out - whatever makes the most sense for your industry, your business and your team.

- *Now develop Some Key Metrics:* Be ambitious and be bold. As author Jim Collins suggested, it is okay to develop BHAG (Big Hairy Audacious Goals). Such goals could include targets for size, revenues, profitability, number of customers, number of employees, number of cities or countries you will be in - you get the idea. It is said that when we commit to such goals with fervor and work towards them with all our abilities and intent, the universe appears to come to our aid.
- *Then make a list of the Key Challenges.* There will always be challenges and by writing them down you are taking the first step towards addressing them. Some of them, like most worries, will never come to fruition, but others will need to be resolved.

Vision – there it is, all on one page. To develop this takes time. My clients have to prepare for this meeting in advance and come ready with their thoughts, doubts and questions. We then spend an entire day to develop this first page as a team. Thoughts are built upon, pursued, discarded, reassembled and then finally embraced. The final product becomes *our* product; nobody remembers who championed what. The best results come about when every single member of the team feels that *they did it.*

Every time I have done this with clients, friends, or mentees, it has been a productive exercise. People sometimes struggle with the purpose, especially in established businesses. However, my guess is that entrepreneurs will not. The values exercise is a challenge and there is a tendency to give others a pass. Be careful. If you do not currently embody a value, put it down under issues, or make it someone's task to think about how to develop that quality within the organization. *Culture is ultimately defined by action, not words, especially the actions of the leader.*

The long-term goals excite people. It gives them a reason for all the hard work and emotion they put into the business. Do not be afraid to think big. I have always liked Robert Browning's exhortation: *"Ah, but a man's reach should exceed his grasp, Or what's a heaven for?"*

Execution

As the Vision's heady aroma permeates the senses, it is now time to tune in Jack Welch: *"Good business leaders create a vision, articulate the vision, passionately own the vision, and relentlessly drive it to completion."* It is time to get into the more mundane, nitty gritty act of actually getting things done and drive relentlessly towards completion.

On the second page of the VET you will capture the one-year plan, 90-day plan, 30-day tasks and the issues that need to be resolved. Let's take a look at the key components.

<u>Execution</u>: VET – Page 2

Quarter Ending:

1-YEAR PLAN ENDING:	MONTHLY: ROCKS		ISSUES LIST (by Priority)
Key Goals: 1. 2. 3. **Key Metrics:** 1. 2. 3. **For the Quarter:** **Key Goals:** 1. 2. 3. **Key Metrics:** 1. 2. 3.	**Rocks** are Tasks / Priorities that must be accomplished – beyond day-to-day work – that will allow the team to meet its monthly, quarterly and annual goals. Each team member will have about 3 rocks per month. The 5 most important rocks for the month are put on this sheet. All other rocks should be listed on a separate sheet and monitored weekly.		1. 2. 3. 4. 5. 6. 7.

Rock Descriptions		Who
1.		
2.		
3.		
4.		
5.		

One Year Plan: From the longer-term perspective, you must move to the upcoming 12 months. At this stage you may not have total clarity about everything that needs to get done this year and how you will do it. Nevertheless, it is important to make estimates. The components of the one-year plan are:

> *Key Metrics:* These can include, but need not be limited to: sales and profit targets and other measurables (e.g. customer acquisition targets, fund raising targets, start up dates, etc.)
> *Key Goals:* State the three key things the business must achieve this year to achieve the long term goals. This could include launching a product by a certain date, acquiring a certain share of market or distribution, developing a key customer relationship etc.

90-day Plan: This is where you focus on closer goals. What must you accomplish within the next 3 months? These will be subsets of the one-year plan. Bigger goals get chunked into smaller, more digestible pieces. You will use the same format as above.

> *3 Key Goals to help achieve the one-year goal*
> *3 Key Metrics*

30-day Plan: Are you starting to see a pattern here? We hope so. In this segment, each team member will take three tasks that they are committed to finishing in the next 30 days. These are specific priorities that must be accomplished in order for the team to meet its 90-day goals. It is the smaller pieces that add up to the bigger whole.

In *Get A Grip,* Gino Wickman[11] calls these "rocks." He explains that if you have a bucket and fill it with sand (your day-to-day work), there may not be room to put in the rocks. Therefore, put the rocks in first and only then fill your bucket with the sand that is absolutely necessary. The key thought is that each team member must deliver on these "rocks" in addition to their day-to-day responsibilities. It is the accomplishment of these priorities / rocks that will ensure the success of the plan.

> *Why Three?* Each team member should take three rocks. A long list is a surefire recipe for a lack of focus and getting very little accomplished. Can this number vary? Of course, use your common sense! But the intent is for team members to complete **all** their rocks, always.

Weekly Meetings and Issues Resolution

Keep a running list of all the issues. This ensures that everyone's concerns have been heard. Then prioritize them. Over time, teams get good at working through these issues expeditiously.

Wickman in *Get A Grip* suggests a process of resolving the issues called IDS (Issues - Discussion - Solution). It sounds like a relatively simple model, but the reality is that teams rarely solve issues; rather they go in circles without a resolution. They end up leaving the meetings frustrated and unclear on the next steps.

Wickman's key insight is that the stated reason for the issue is rarely the real reason. The team must dig into the question and find out what the *real issue* is. What is truly blocking you or bothering you? It takes digging below the surface to discover what really needs to be done and then to ask the questions: why is it not being done, what needs to be done, when and who will do it? As the team develops and forms stronger bonds, such conversations get easier and more productive.

A start up business needs to have such meetings at least once or twice a week. Productive meetings require a disciplined approach; below are guidelines that we have seen work.

---

[11] Wickman, Gino. *Get a Grip.* Dallas: BenBella Books, 2012.

71

Guidelines

- Always have the meetings on a pre-set day and time, for example every Tuesday at 9 am.
- They should be approximately 60-90 minutes long. To truly work as a team, you must spend the time to develop the trust and learn to dig deeper to solve the issues. This actually reduces the work and frees up time.
- Always start and end the meeting on time.
- Pick one of the team members to act as a moderator. They will be responsible for keeping the team on track and on time. Switch moderators every two or three months.

The Agenda should always be the same - see sample below. Turn off all cell phones. We have assumed that meetings will be 75-minutes.

1. *9 - 9:05 am: Catching up, random banter.*
2. *9:05 - 9:10 am: Check status of the tasks from the last meeting. Presumably everything got done. (These tasks will generally be short-term action steps.)*
3. *9:10 - 9:20 am: Any new issue since the last meeting?*
4. *9:20 - 9:25 am: Rocks check - Team members are you on or off track? If off track, do you need help? If yes, add to the issues list.*
5. *9:25- 10:05 am: Issues Resolution.*
6. *10:05 - 10:10 am: List and assign any tasks from this meeting.*
7. *10:10 - 10:15 am: Wrap up. Rate the meeting on a 1-5 scale (1 = Terrible, 5 = Very Productive). Keep track of these ratings and note the progress.*

When addressing issues:
- Look at the issues list and prioritize them.
- Start with Issue #1. *You will keep working on an issue until it is resolved.*
- Resolution means a) issue understood, b) issue really understood, c) action plan determined, d) assigned to someone with a clear expectation of what is required by when. Sometimes issues are raised that the company may have no control over, for example melting glaciers or dwindling rain forests. If you feel deeply about such an issue, put that on your personal agenda and work on it in your spare time.
- This process may at times be frustrating because the progress appears to be slow. However, jumping from one unresolved issue to a new one will end up being both unproductive and unsatisfying.
- At the 40-minute mark, stop regardless of where you are.

Once A Month: Have a 4-hour meeting to discuss rocks and issues in depth. Evaluate how you did on your rocks. Develop new ones for the next 30 days.

Once A Quarter: Update the 90-day plan, have a more thorough discussion on the results and rocks. Take one day. (Quite often in my one-day client meetings 30 issues may end up being scribbled on the blackboard. By the end of the day, virtually all issues will have been discussed, action plans decided upon and some issues will have been dropped.)

Once A Year: Update Vision and develop a new Annual Plan. This will require two days, one for the Vision and one for the plan for the upcoming year.

Getting things done is a discipline. It is not easy, but with a bit of practice, it becomes a habit. The method and calendar laid out will help you get what you need to get done. Embrace it, practice it, tweak it if necessary, but move ahead and *get things done.*

What have I learned from the sessions I have facilitated? Keeping on track is hard. People meander. The facilitator does not want to cut off people because he works with them and is worried about damaging relationships. Consider getting an outside facilitator for your quarterly and annual meetings. If you adhere to the strict 75 minutes for the weekly meetings, sooner or later someone will get frustrated with the indiscipline and demand a change. Make them the facilitator, then support them by being disciplined.

Assignment: Develop Your Team's VET

VISION: VET – Page 1

Purpose	
5 Year Key Measurables (Maybe 3)	
Values: (Max 5)	
1. Problem / Solution	**The Five Filters**
2. Product / Service	
3. Customer	
4. Competition	
5. Business Model	
Key Challenges (Max 5)	

EXECUTION – VET – PAGE 2

One YEAR – **3 Key Goals**	
One YEAR – **3 Key Metrics**	
QUARTER – **3 Key Goals**	
QUARTER – **3 Key Metrics**	
Teammate #1 **Quarter Rocks**	
Teammate #2 **Quarter Rocks**	
Teammate #3 **Quarter Rocks**	
Teammate #4 **Quarter Rocks**	
Key Challenges	

Values Development Exercise

1. Develop your list of values after a vigorous discussion.
2. Now, evaluate: Yes or No or Maybe.

Values	Team Member #1	Team Member #2	Team Member #3	Team Member #4
1.				
2.				
3.				
4.				
5.				

Note: Values are only meaningful if the team members practice them. If there are some values that some team members get an "N" in, then either a) the team member must learn to adhere to the value, or b) the value needs to be dropped, or c) the team member must leave the team.

Suggested Meetings Schedule

1. **Weekly Level 10 Meeting**: Be sure to rate each meeting on a scale of 1-10, and keep track of these scores.

2. **Once A Month**: Have a 4-hour meeting to discuss rocks and issues in depth. Evaluate how you did on your rocks.

3. **Once A Quarter**: Update the 90-day plan, have a more thorough discussion on the results and rocks. Take one day.

4. **Once A Year**: Update Vision and develop a new Annual Plan. This will require two days, one for the Vision and one for the plan for the upcoming year.

Don't meander like the rest of the world and then wonder what might have been. Follow this discipline and You will EXECUTE!

Additional Notes

Chapter 6

BUSINESS MODEL
&
PLAN B

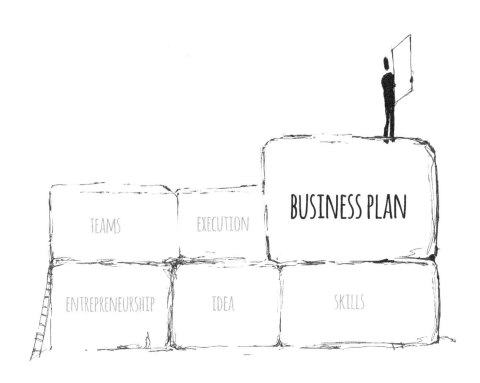

"I started the business with a simple question: How can we make the process of buying a computer better? The answer was: Sell computers directly to the end customer. Eliminate the reseller's markup and pass those savings on to the customer." - Michael Dell, Direct from Dell

"The future of TOMS is really creating a whole new business model of this one-for-one giving and expanding the TOMS model from shoes into other products as well." - Blake Mycoskie

"Small retail shops selling bags of freshly ground coffee are not what made Starbucks a household word. And an effective free search tool is not what made the word Google a verb nor made billions for Google's investors. Both of these now-global brands owe their success not to their Plan A, but to Plan B." - Mullins & Komisar[12], Getting to Plan B

~~~~~~~~

Key Topics in this Chapter

- What is a Business Model?

- Generating Revenues

- Costs

- Capital Needed

- Break-even Point

- Operating Model

- Plan B – The Need To Pivot

- Assignment: Understand your Business Model

---

[12] Mullins and Komisar. *Getting to Plan B – Breaking Through To A Better Business Model.* Boston: Harvard Business School Publishing, 2009

What is a Business Model?

At one level, a business model answers the question: "How will the business make money?" Beyond that it is also an idea, process, strategy and an insight that results in value creation for the customers and profits for the enterprise.

IBM, HP, Compaq and others were selling personal and business computers before Michael Dell thought of a new idea while sitting in his dorm room. He reasoned that costs could be reduced by selling directly to the customer and eliminating middlemen like Best Buy. The customer would pay at the time of ordering the computer. This money would be used to finance the inventory. By ordering the exact inventory required, the risk of obsolescence would be reduced. The resulting lower costs could then be passed on to the customer, which would lead to higher sales. This, in a nutshell, was Dell's business model - new, clean, efficient and elegant.

What was Starbuck's initial business model? It started off selling upscale coffee beans then pivoted to delivering an experience. It was a high quality, highly customized iteration of coffee and milk in a friendly environment. That is why Howard Schultz coined it "a third space" away from home and work. This allowed them to charge $4 for a product where the ingredient cost of coffee, milk and a paper cup added up to about $0.60.

Without the aid of any business books, The Grateful Dead developed a very successful business model in the 1960s and became one of the top grossing bands without ever having a number one hit. Since they did not like working with the record labels, they concentrated on doing live concerts where they encouraged people to record their music for free. They made their money from selling concert tickets, clothing and other paraphernalia to their intensely devoted following of Deadheads.

The profit component is an important part of the business model. Without profits, a business cannot survive for long; the law of financial gravity inevitably reasserts itself. New business models put pressure and sometimes obsolete even seemingly strong businesses. Newspapers are a current example of such obsolescence underway.

"Newspapers with declining circulations can complain all they want about their readers and even say they have no taste. But you will still go out of business over time. A newspaper is not a public trust - it has a business model that either works or it doesn't." - Marc Andreessen

The *financial* purpose of any business is to make money. You sell a product or service for a certain price, which creates *Revenues*. You incur *Costs* to generate these revenues. The difference between the two is *Profit*.

Revenue - Costs = Profit

This is the *fundamental equation* of a business. Making a profit is a necessary condition for a business to survive. Yes, there are a few details involved, but this is the basis of profitability.

A business model helps us examine and understand the key elements of the financial equation: how the revenues will be generated, what it will cost to provide the service, what support (overhead) structure will be required and how much capital will be needed to start the business. The goal is to both understand these factors and to find ways to improve the model.

This information will be examined in much greater detail in later chapters. For now, our goal is to understand these concepts at a high level. From time to time some numbers will be involved. Some of you may have a fear of numbers, do not worry. Everything is presented in the simplest way possible.

Generating Revenues

Revenue (or sales) is the money generated by selling a product or service. Without revenues can a business exist? In the vast majority of cases, *no.* There are some startup exceptions, especially in Silicon Valley, where businesses are funded in the hopes of hitting a home run later. Instagram and Snapchat are recent examples of this phenomenon but are rare instances.

There are many ways to generate revenues:

Selling Units: A grocery store on average carries 20,000 items such as food products, toiletries, medicines etc. There you will find many products from P&G including shampoos, toothpaste, Gillette blades, laundry detergents and so on. Each of these products is sold as a unit. P&G sells these units to the grocery stores, which in turn sells them to people like us.

Services: Doctors, plumbers, accountants and lawyers are examples of businesses providing a service.

Advertising: Newspapers and magazines make most of their money from selling advertising in their publications. Google makes 90% of its revenues from advertising.

Licensing: Software companies like Microsoft and Adobe generate revenues by licensing their products to companies and individuals.

Franchising: Examples include McDonald's, Burger King, Subway and H&R Block tax services.

Subscription: Virtually all newspapers and magazines, including *The Wall Street Journal, New York Times, New Yorker* and *Vogue* generate part of their revenues from subscriptions. Netflix and Spotify also generate all their revenues in this manner.

Memberships: Examples include Costco, Sam's Club and many museums.

Intermediary: eBay is an excellent example of a company that generates revenues by being an intermediary between buyers and sellers.

Transactions: A real estate broker only gets paid when a transaction is completed. Schwab makes money when an investor buys or sells a stock.

Do not get hung up on the exact classification such as whether Netflix is a subscription or a membership service. Just understand that there are many ways to generate revenues. Businesses often combine several of these sources.

- Amazon sells units (books) and has a subscription service (Amazon Prime). It is also experimenting with a new same day delivery service.
- Microsoft licenses software, sells Xbox and also sells a monthly Xbox membership service.
- The *Wall Street Journal* sells newspapers through annual subscriptions and daily unit sales. They also sell advertising.
- eBay provides both an online intermediary service and a payment service through PayPal.
- Costco sells products but makes most of its profits from memberships.
Bottom line, by mixing and matching different processes there are a variety of ways to generate revenue.
In considering revenues, you must not only think about the units you will sell, but also the *selling price.*

There is no exact formula to determine the right price. While competitive prices can provide a barometer, the fundamental factor is the value perceived by the user of your product. Hence The Wall Street Journal is more expensive than the Chicago Tribune, an iPhone is more expensive than a Nokia phone, the Economist magazine is more expensive than Time magazine and the price of a pair of jeans can vary widely based on the brand, even though the cost to produce these products may be the same.

Existing businesses also must reexamine their prices periodically. Many consumer items go up in price with inflation. Some products continue to add real or perceived value and are priced accordingly. A Gillette blade that sold for $0.25 some years ago now retails for $4 as the technology continues to improve. As I write this book, I note that the Amazon Prime Subscription price is going up from $79 per year to $99 and Netflix is also increasing its monthly subscription fees.

Costs

There are two broad categories of costs: *Cost of Goods* and *Operating Expenses.*

Cost of Goods is the cost directly related to the product or service. For example, the cost for a pair of jeans at Costco would be the cost of buying the jeans from the manufacturer plus the labor cost that was incurred in selling it to you.

Operating Expenses are the expenses beyond the above costs. For Costco, this would include advertising, utilities, accounting and legal fees, salaries for its buyers and management, leasing and other costs.

Subtracting Costs of Goods from Revenue gives us the Gross Margin. From this we subtract Operating Expenses to calculate the *Profit* (before taxes). A business must evaluate each element of cost and try to reduce it wherever possible while providing the level of service that it desires to offer.

Capital Needed

To start a business, you will need *Start Up* capital before you have even made your first sale. Money will be needed for several things and this list will vary by type of business. Items may include costs to develop your product, legal and accounting fees, marketing help, website development, getting patents, etc. The business itself may need to be underwritten for some time before it becomes profitable. Think of these costs as *start up* costs.

Once the business gets rolling there are two other key needs for capital.

1. *Working Capital:* This is the money that is needed to run the day-to-day business. There are three key components: *Receivables,* which is money that people owe you, *Payables,* which is the money that you owe others and *Inventory,* which can be in the form of finished goods or raw materials.

    Let's start with *Receivables.* Assume you are a small winery selling to wine distributors and you have to give them 60 day terms, meaning they will pay you 60 days after they receive the wine. (These terms are negotiated between the parties, but size and industry practices often determine such terms.) This is a *Receivable* on your book because the money is owed to you and you anticipate receiving it.

    In turn, you have to pay your suppliers in 30 days for the glass bottles and the grapes you buy from them. This becomes a *Payable* on your books.

    In addition to this, let us assume that you will need to keep 1000 cases of wine in *Inventory* to be able to fill the orders as they come in. This too will cost money.

    In this example, you will receive the cash from receivables in 60 days, but you have to clear up your payables in 30 days. Hence you will need money to fund this gap. In addition, you will need money to fund the inventories that you stock. These are the three main things you will need to monitor and fund on a day-to-day basis. This is called *Working Capital.*

2. *Fixed Assets:* You also may need to buy equipment such as computers, cars and perhaps even land to build the winery. This capital is called *Fixed Assets.*

Admittedly, these factors have been simplified, but they are adequate to understand the concepts being discussed.

Break-Even Point

A business will only break-even when the revenues equal the costs. In the case of your winery, you will need to know how many cases of wine must be sold for the business to earn enough money to equal the costs. This tells you the break-even volume (quantity). The other important component is the time it will take to reach this breakeven point. These two numbers of breakeven, volume and time, let you calculate how much money you will need to get to profitability. The larger the amount and the longer the time frame, the riskier the project. (It may also create the most value.)

Operating Models

Another way to think about business models is to look at the strategies of pricing, volume and service being deployed.

- Walmart and McDonald's have a *Low Price, Low Margin, High Volume* model. They sell products at a low price, their profit margins are low and therefore they must generate high volumes (meaning they must sell a lot of products to a lot of people) to achieve profitability.
- The Ritz Carlton and Neiman Marcus have a *High Price, High Margin and High Service* model. Their prices are steep, but they offer exceptional service which requires high overhead costs. The Ritz Carlton will serve far fewer customers than a Holiday Inn, but they will make a satisfactory profit because of their higher margins.
- Most other models fall somewhere in between.

You must choose a model that best fits what you are offering and what your customers want. You also need to determine which key customers you will focus on. When you try to serve and please everybody, you end up not pleasing anyone.

Let's look at Costco and Whole Foods to understand their models and financial performance. *

For Fiscal Year 2014	Costco	Whole Foods
Sales (Billions of $)	$113	$14
As a % of Sales		
Gross Margin (%)	13%	36%
Operating Expenses (%)	-10%	-29%
Operating Margin (%)	3%	7%
Fixed Assets (%)	13%	21%

Costco has annual sales of $113 billion while Whole Foods is much smaller, but still does a very respectable $14 billion.

Costco prides itself in providing very attractive prices: hence it keeps prices low, which result in a low Gross Margin of only 13%. It must therefore keep its Operating Expenses very, very, low at 10%. This leads to an Operating Margin of 3%. Because it has high sales / store, its fixed asset / sales ratio is only 13%, which means that it generates $100 of sales for $13 of fixed assets. Costco is an excellent example of a low price, low margin and high volume business.

*All data from Yahoo Finance

Whole Foods provides high quality natural products at a relatively higher price. They earn a Gross Margin of 36%, but they also provide a higher level of service which costs 29%, resulting in an Operating Margin of 7%. Because it has many smaller stores it needs $21 of fixed capital to support $100 of sales.

Both of these companies are profitable and do a good job meeting the differing needs of their customers. *The point to be underscored is that there are many ways to develop profitable business models.*

Let's look at one more example. Apple is mostly a hardware company, albeit an upscale hardware company. Its Gross Margin is 39%, but because it outsources most of its production, its Operating Expense is only 10%, giving it an Operating Margin of 29%.

Microsoft, in contrast, is a software company with a high Gross Margin of 69% despite wasting a ton of money on its extraneous businesses. With its bloated bureaucracy, Operating Expenses are 37%, but this still delivers a very healthy Operating Margin of 32%.

One is a hardware company and the other a software company. Both find ways to serve their customers while making a lot of money in the process. The trick is to find the business model that will work for *you*, while deeply satisfying *your* customer.

Plan B – The Need To Pivot

Starting plans for most businesses, (let's call them Plan A) rarely work. Harvard Professor, Amar Bhide, some years back, explained that 93% of successful companies had to pivot (a fancy way to say change, adjust, modify, or start from scratch) and alter their business plans to achieve success. When you start a business you make assumptions, but it is the marketplace that determines what will work and what will not work. Be flexible and accept that you may have to pivot a few times before the universe smiles upon your venture and your model starts to click.

Now here is the good news: pivoting is often a way to recombine the same resources in a different manner. You may need to develop a new focus, a new customer target, or offer a different bundle of value. Iterate and pivot is the byword. There are very few, if any, truly new ideas. You do not have to be a genius to create a new business model if the current one comes up short.

> *There is no such thing as a new idea. It is impossible. We simply take a lot of old ideas and put them into a sort of mental kaleidoscope. We give them a turn and they make new and curious combinations. We keep on turning and making new combinations indefinitely; but they are the same old pieces of colored glass that have been in use through all the ages. - Mark Twain, a Biography*

Getting to Plan B – Breaking Through To A Better Business Model by Mullins and Komisar, is a book I use in my class and I highly recommend it. The authors detail stories of several well-known and less well-known companies as they pivoted multiple times until their model finally worked.

For example, the story of eBay is well known as the founder created a program to sell some of his girlfriend's junk. Along the way it morphed into the now famous company. PayPal started as cryptography software. It pivoted to enabling cash transfers on a PalmPilot before ending up being the cash transfer vehicle on the web. Consider Apple – how many times has it pivoted after its near death experience? Today it makes most of its money from phones not computers.

Getting to Plan B offers four key points that will help you improve your business idea as you do your inevitable pivots.

1. *Analogs*: If you see a company doing something you like, see if that idea can fit into your business. There are good ideas everywhere. Embrace them. You do not need to reinvent the wheel. Napster was perhaps an analog for iTunes. It showed that people were willing to download music from the web. When they finally got around to it, Google discovered its analog in advertising. The coffee shops in Italy were the analog for Howard Schultz's Starbucks. He saw that the customers were regulars and thought of the coffee

shop as a home away from home. This gave him the idea to create the environment within Starbucks that he did.

2. *Antilogs:* Perhaps you have a highly unfavorable reaction to what you see a company is doing. Never fear, this too is a gift. Terrible ideas are everywhere; compose a list and make sure to take a different path. The antilog for iTunes was the behavior of record companies that forced customers to buy an entire album, even if they only wanted one or two tracks. Starbucks was one of the first companies to offer health insurance to part time employees. Here is the antilog: this came about because Mr. Schultz, in his youth, had seen his father not get medical help when he was injured and it bothered him immensely. Are Spotify and Pandora the impending antilogs to iTunes and Sirius XM to all radio commercials?

3. *Leaps Of Faith:* There are times (actually many) when data is just not available and you have to make a leap of faith. The Leap of Faith for iTunes was that record companies would allow their music to be sold at a flat rate of $0.99 per track. Spotify had to believe that people would be willing to pay for a vast library of music on a monthly basis. Whole Foods had to assume that people would be willing to pay more for organic food. Starbucks, at launch time, had to believe that customers would be willing to pay three to four times more for good coffee and a nice environment than they were used to paying at McDonald's and Dunkin Donuts.

4. *Dashboard:* This is a way of compiling all your LOFs (Leaps of Faith) on a sheet of paper and assiduously testing them in the marketplace. Some of the LOFs will work and others will not, but all need to be verified by real customers in the marketplace.

In my last class, the teams took the notion of pivoting to heart. Of the seven projects, three were totally discarded (which is quite a pivot), while one was modified significantly. The end result was better business propositions than I had ever seen before.

This is a good framework to use as you develop your business model and as you pivot from one letter of the alphabet to the next. Keep going until you find just the right one.

Assignment: Understand Your Business Model

Sometimes the fields of accounting and finance can make these concepts very complicated. Learn to focus on the basic principles and you will do fine.

You will explore all of these aspects in much greater detail in Part 2 and 3 of the book. Getting started now, even with rough assumptions, will give you a better handle on your business idea, business model, what you know and what you do not know but need to find out. A bit of trepidation is not uncommon, but that is when we must summon Joseph Conrad:

"Facing it, always facing it, that's the way to get through. Face it."

The following template is designed to help you collect your thoughts. Take the time to complete it. Now you have a foundation. In the next section we will move towards focusing on the customer, the source of all revenues. Rough back of the envelope calculations are fine.

Business Model Template: Next 12 Months

Unit Sales	
Revenue (Unit Sales x Selling Price)	$
Cost of Goods	$
Operating Expenses: List all your key items and add up the total.	$
Profit (Revenues – Cost of Goods – Operating Expenses)	$
Are you profitable? Yes? Great! If not, revisit your idea and tweak as necessary.	
How <u>many months</u> will it take to breakeven?	
How many <u>units</u> must you sell to breakeven?	
How much money will you need to get started?	$
How will you raise this money? (Savings, Family & Friends, Kickstarter, Loans etc.)	
Analogs:	
Antilogs:	
Leaps of Faith:	
Dashboard:	

Additional Notes

Part II

CUSTOMER

A business exists to serve a customer. In this segment you will focus on understanding your customer in depth. You will learn the 3P / 3C marketing model, understand how value is created, who your competition is and what is unique about your business. You will move ahead and develop a brand and a pricing strategy. You will then determine what channels of distribution you will employ and learn the art of selling. By the end, having a great understanding of your customer will give you adequate knowledge and data to flush out your initial marketing plan.

Chapter 7

INTRODUCTION TO MARKETING

"The aim of marketing is to know and understand the customer so well the product or service fits him and sells itself." - Peter Drucker

"The best marketing strategy ever: CARE" - Gary Vaynerchuk

"Your brand is a story unfolding across all customer touch points." - Jonah Sachs

~~~~~~~~

Key Topics in this Chapter

- A Simple Marketing Model

- Fieldwork for You

- Sample Assignment: Chipotle (*Digging Deeper*)

- How to Do Research

- Assignment: Develop Your 3Ps and 3Cs

A Simple Marketing Model

Billions of dollars are spent on marketing each year, but much of it is wasted. How many of you watch TV commercials? When was the last time a billboard or a newspaper ad caught your attention? How fast do you toss out junk mail? The word "junk" says it all.

Why do you think so much marketing spending is futile? Simply because most companies focus on *selling* something and not on what the customer wants. Companies need to reverse course.

Marketing is about the customer, meeting *his* needs and wants. This can only be done by understanding these needs in depth. You may even have to go further. Today many more people are looking to do business with organizations that share their values and ethos. The mission of Warby Parker or Patagonia may resonate with you. Or perhaps it is the companies that focus on green, organic, Fair Trade or Non GMO products that you feel more deeply about. We buy from people we like and there is a strong social and emotional element to our decisions.

Professor Gretchen Dobie, who has been teaching an introductory marketing class to MBA students at Loyola University for many years, puts it this way: *"Effective marketing is recognizing customer needs and devising ways to attract customers to the product."*

Marketing, then, is both a strategy and a variety of tactics. The latter include advertising, promoting, pricing, branding, positioning, segmenting and selling. However, the best place to start is to focus on the basic questions that were raised earlier:

- What is the problem that is being solved? Who is the customer? How much will they pay?
- Who is the competition? Why will customers buy your product over those of the competition?

Professor Dobie gives my students an introduction to marketing, a crash course of sorts. This chapter is based significantly on that class where we use a modified marketing model that we call "The 3Ps and 3Cs."

The 3 Ps

- *PRODUCT* - What is the product?

    Products can be a physical good (iPhone), person (Kobe Bryant advertising sneakers), place (Disneyland), organization (Red Cross), service (Verizon), or even an idea (Breast Cancer ribbon).

- *PRICE* - At what price will the product be sold?

    A customer receives a bundle of benefits in every transaction. For example, Chipotle is a place to go to get somewhat higher quality Mexican food. The total value that a customer receives at Chipotle includes the product, the service (speed, mode of assembly, cleanliness, friendliness etc.) and also Chipotle's philosophy of local sourcing and its humane approach to animals.

    It is the customer's perception that determines the value to him and the price he is willing to pay, not what the company actually thinks, believes, markets, or portrays.

- *PROMOTION* - How will the product be promoted?

    Typically, promotions have several components such as Advertising, Sales Promotion, Personal Selling and Publicity.

    Advertising includes commercials on TV and radio, advertising in newspapers, magazines, billboards and direct mail. Digitally, web sites, podcasts, webinars, email blasts, banner ads and social media are all options.

    Sales Promotion includes coupons, displays in stores, demonstrations and in-store sampling (like you see at Costco).

    Personal Selling would include hiring salespeople, agents, distributors, telemarketing and selling at trade shows.

Publicity entails getting the news about the company, or the product, to the customers. An article written about the product is desirable. Speaking on a panel provides publicity too.

Word of Mouth is the oldest and by the far the best form of promotion. However, going viral is its ultimate manifestation.

The 3 Cs

- *COMPETITION* - Which other companies sell something similar to the same customers? For example, the competition for Chipotle would be Qdoba, Baja Fresh and maybe even Panera depending on how broadly you defined the competitive arena.

- *CONSUMER* - Who is the target market for the product? You need to know their demographics (such as age, sex, income, education, etc.), as well as their psychographics (beliefs, causes they feel strongly about, etc.).

- *CHANNEL* - What are the channels of distribution, specifically where will the product be available?

    Domino's, the pizza chain, has two key channels - *home delivery* and *store pickups* for example.

    Starbucks' main channel of distribution is through its retail locations. They also sell their products in grocery and convenience stores.

    Let's assume Kellogg's wants to sell you Frosted Flakes. After manufacturing it, they ship the boxes to a wholesaler who then sends it to retailers (Safeway, Vons, Jewel, etc.). You then buy this box of cereal from your local retailer.

    Amazon works an e-commerce model, selling directly to consumers.

    There are other channels such as telemarketing, home-delivery through online services and much less frequently of late - Tupperware parties.

Using this simple model, you can learn a significant amount about a company, its products, pricing and competitive strength among other things.

Fieldwork for You

It's time for a field trip so you can experiment with this model. I hope you're hungry. This is the same assignment that Professor Dobie gives my class.

Your assignment is to visit a Chipotle restaurant and look for the physical "plant," customers, menu and the atmosphere. Based upon your visit only (no internet or other type of research) define each of the Ps and Cs and detail how you arrived at the decision. I am interested in the reasons behind your thoughtful answers. In addition, have you seen or experienced any marketing by Chipotle that has really resonated with you? If so, what made it significant to you?

With more than 1500 locations, I suspect there is a Chipotle near you. No excuses will be accepted. It is time to get a burrito or a salad. Guacamole is optional.

Do not look at the next section until you complete this "feeding yourself" mission.

What did you find? Do you have your notes handy? Without knowing it, perhaps you are on your way to becoming a marketer.

Sample Assignment: Chipotle – Digging Deeper

Professor Dobie makes the following observations for Chipotle in our class.

The 3 Ps

1. *PRODUCT:* There are four main items: Burritos, Tacos, Burrito Bowls and Salad Bowls.

2. *PRICE:* Most of their products are priced around $6 with the total meal costing approximately $10.

3. *PROMOTION:* Chipotle appears to do very limited promotions. They do not have any national advertising of any significance. They do have billboards in some locations. Occasionally they run promotions around Halloween or events tied to local markets such as college football games. Most of their promotion comes from word of mouth.

The 3 Cs

1. *COMPETITION:* Who is Chipotle's competition? At one level, every dollar consumed on food - be it at home or in a restaurant - vies for the same spending and meal occasion. However, let us make the assumption that the consumer has decided to eat out and is looking for either a quick meal or Mexican food.

    A focus on a quick meal would lead us to the fast food industry. Within this segment, there are restaurants that serve things "as is," like McDonald's. Then there are the restaurants that will customize your order like Panera and Chipotle. Let's call the first group, McDonald's and Taco Bell, "Fast Food" or "Quick Service" and the customizers like Chipotle and Panera, "Fast Casual."

    So now who are Chipotle's competitors? In the "Mexican" segment, there are companies like Qdoba, Baja Fresh, Rubio's and Moe's.

    In the "Fast Casual" segment, there are chains such as Panera, Potbelly and Five Guys.

    The most important question while looking at the competition is: what is the point of difference? As you think about your product be sure to ask *"What is the bundle of benefits we are providing that is superior to the competition?"*

2. *CONSUMER:* Who eats at Chipotle? From your visit you can make a few guesses.

You can strengthen your guesses by doing further research (discussed in the section below). Using research mainly from the web, Professor Dobie has developed the following data for Chipotle.
Demographics:

- 60% Female, 40% Male
- Age 18-34
- Income $10-60K per year
- 82% Caucasian
- 44% College Educated
- 69% Have no children

Psychographics:

- Environmentally conscious
- Active lifestyle
- Socially focused
- Tech savvy
- Image conscious
- Financially focused

Now can you start to visualize these customers? My students are invariably staunch customers of Chipotle and maybe you are too. Are you getting a clearer idea of the consumer?

3. *CHANNELS:* In the case of Chipotle, the location itself is the channel of distribution since the food is consumed on the premises or carried out.

This model can help you understand the landscape of the industry, the key competitors and the consumers, thereby, allowing you to start formulating your point of difference. What will you offer that will provide meaningful differentiation and make you successful?

How to do Research

As you look at the 3Ps and 3Cs, it is evident that you will need to research many of the answers. A good way to do this is by hypothesizing answers wherever possible and then doing research to validate your assumptions. You may end up changing your initial thinking or verifying it.

The more important research is likely to be the work that entails direct interaction with the customers. Let's call this primary research.

Talking to potential customers or observing them use your product will give you the greatest insight. Do not be afraid to engage people. Do so politely. People generally want to help. The more direct the feedback, the richer the data will be.

One of the student teams had come up with an idea of an app that could be used at the airport to order food as people waited in the TSA lines. To get data to validate their hypothesis, they needed to talk to frequent travelers and airport restaurants. They were not sure how to approach the latter, but then realized that one of our guest speakers was a vice president of such a chain. A quick call to her elicited an introduction. The airport restaurant was quite willing to listen to their idea, critique it, offer suggestions and share data. Suddenly the hypothesis started to become real and before long it became a viable idea.

In this day and age of communicating via technology, the greatest area of untapped knowledge is a conversation with a real human being. Try it. You might be pleasantly surprised.

Another form of primary research is surveys, either through email or an online service such as SurveyMonkey. A strong response on a survey can provide good validation. If the idea is not resonating with people, you can either change the idea or see if there is a better way to explain your idea. Listening to potential customers is important, perhaps critical. Very few of us have the gift of just knowing what people want as Steve Jobs did.

The secondary research sources include Google, company websites, libraries, Census, periodicals and reports from a variety of sources. Your challenge will not be a dearth of information. Instead, it will be making sense of the data, focusing on what is truly being said and not hearing only what you want to hear.

"To understand how consumers really think and feel, it is vital to go beyond words." - *Katja Bressette.*

That is a challenge worthy of you.

Assignment: Develop Your 3Ps & 3C

The 3 Ps

- What is your Product or Service?

- What is your Price? And, why is it a good value for the customer?

- What marketing mix of Promotions will your company use?

The 3 Cs

- Who is your Competition?

- Who is your Consumer?

Describe in detail your consumer's demographics (such as age, sex, income, education, etc.)

Describe in detail their psychographics (beliefs, causes they feel strongly about, etc.)

•   **What Channels will you use to distribute your product?**

"Good marketing makes the company look smart. Great marketing makes the customer feel smart." - Joe Chernov

Make your customer feel smart. Better yet, connect with them in a deep way. It's time to make your idea come alive.

Additional Notes

Chapter 8

THE VALUE PROPOSITION

"We brought prices down, down, down so they are now essentially commodities. So if we want to succeed in this business, we have to move in a direction of adding other value to the relationship with our clients. And so where I might have said 15 years ago, 'We want to be the best discount brokerage,' today I want to be the best 'relationship company' in financial services." - Charles Schwab

"We need to stop interrupting what people are interested in and be what people are interested in." - Craig Davis, former Chief Creative Officer at J. Walter Thompson

"There are multiple ways to be externally focused that are very successful. You can be customer-focused or competitor-focused. Some people are internally focused, and if they reach critical mass, they can tip the whole company." - Jeff Bezos

~~~~~~~~

Key Topics in this Chapter

- What is Value?

- What is the job that the product is being hired for?

- Marketing Utility

- Disneyland, Nike and more

- The Utility Equation

- Assignment: What is the Utility of your product?

Understanding customers and connecting with them is the essence of marketing. Such understanding is hard to come by since human beings are complex creatures. They say one thing and do something else. They think one way and act another. I always smile when students, dressed in fancy jeans and snazzy sneakers, carrying the latest iPhones, lament their limited means. The reality is that people, including seemingly impoverished students, will always spend money on things they find of value.

What is Value?

You buy a watch to tell time, right? Casio and Rolex both tell time. Which one would you buy and why?

Why does somebody buy a Maserati? It does go fast - very fast - but almost any car can go fast.

Let's take something more basic. A meal at Chipotle costs about $10 and approximately $6 at McDonald's. Are the ingredients at Chipotle that much more expensive? Unlikely. Then why are you willing to pay so much more?

The price of a product represents a bundle of value. What then is the bundle of value of Chipotle that allows it to sell for almost double the price of McDonald's?

Why are people willing to pay $10,000 for a Rolex or $100,000 for a Maserati?

Beauty is in the eyes of the beholder. Value too is in the eyes, mind and heart of the beholder: the customer. How do you go about understanding a customer's bundle of value?

"What is the job that the product is being hired for?"

In the December 2005 *Harvard Business Review*, Harvard Business School Professor Clayton Christensen and his colleagues, tackled this subject in an article titled "Marketing Malpractice."

They suggested that the dry statistics of demographics and psychographics could not fully capture human behavior and motivation. Rather, they posited that each product or service had a *"job to do"* and understanding this job was the key to making the product successful.

The article described the efforts of a large company trying to increase its sales of milkshakes. The company first did a demographic segmentation of the market so it could define the primary milkshake customer. It then experimented with ways to make the milkshake better. They tried making it thicker, thinner, more chocolate, less chocolate and adding fruit. None of these tests led to higher sales.

Professor Christensen and his team took a different tack. They started by observing who used the product, when it was used and why they used it. They learned that the primary consumers of milkshakes in the morning were commuters driving to work who wanted something that would keep them full until lunch. The milkshake was a substitute for eating a bagel or a doughnut in the car and it was far less messy to consume.

With this insight, the company did three things:

1. It created a *thicker* milkshake with chunkier fruit pieces for its morning commuter customers. This took longer to drink and was more filling. The fruit pieces also added a bit of playfulness.
2. A faster pay option was added since these customers were generally in a hurry.
3. At the same time, the company realized that this thicker milkshake was not desirable for children who came in the afternoon with their parents. Did a parent really want to look at their kid sipping a milk shake for 30 minutes? Even parental love has limitations. For this segment, a *thinner* milkshake was created.

The key question that should always be asked is: "What is the job that the product is being hired to do?" Thousands of new products are introduced each year with 95% of them failing. So many products fail because companies focus on products that they can and want to make, rather than on what the customer wants. Renowned Harvard

Marketing Professor Theodore Levitt succinctly captured this idea: *"People don't want to buy a quarter inch drill. They want to make a quarter inch hole."*

"Marketing Malpractice" also offered another key insight: *"With few exceptions, every job that people need or want to do has a social, functional and an emotional dimension."*

These three dimensions, social, functional and emotional, are the bundle of value that we have been searching for.

Marketing Utility

Peter Drucker challenged us to define this *bundle of value* by looking at it from another angle: *What is the purpose of this business to exist?* He felt that there were *only* two key functions of a business: 1) To create a customer, which was done through marketing and 2) To retain the customer by innovating.

So, how does marketing create a customer? Drucker posited: *"By understanding (that) what the customer buys is not just a product or service... It is what the product does for the person."*

Think of the milkshake example above. A milkshake is not just the product but *what it does for the commuter* during his morning drive.

What is the reason for a hospital to exist? Is it to employ doctors and nurses and to create profits for insurance companies? Or is it to heal patients?

What is the purpose of an emergency room? Drucker suggested that people are scared when they come to the emergency room and the goal of the staff should be to provide comfort to the patient quickly. Healing is not only about the medicine but also about the emotions that come with this experience. Have you had to make any such quick trip to the hospital recently?

Last year my wife cut her hand while cooking and the bleeding would not stop. We had to visit the emergency room. It was a weekend and it was not busy. Nevertheless, it took four hours to get an X-ray and get stitches. The staff had perfected the art of looking vaguely interested and utterly bored at the same time. Mr. Drucker would not have been happy and neither were we.

A product does certain things but it is what the product does for *you* where the real value lies. Drucker called this the product's utility. An iPhone is a smartphone that allows you to make calls, text, surf the web, take photographs - the list is endless. But the most important utility of an iPhone is what it says about you, about your tastes and your means. Could these social and emotional feelings be the larger component of the bundle of value?

I have mingled the ideas of Drucker, Levitt and Christensen into what I call *"Marketing Utility."* The combination of the functional, social and emotional elements, in essence, create utility for the customer.

Disneyland, Nike and more

"How many of you have been to Disneyland?" is a question I always ask my classes. Smiles break out, memories are rekindled and a certain joy pervades the room as almost everyone raises their hands. As we discuss what value Disneyland provides, it becomes clear that the *Functional Utility* is pretty low. Rides at Disneyland are interesting but if you wanted thrills you'd be better off going to Six Flags, where the heart is sure to pump faster.

What people remember and value the most about their Disneyland experience is linked to who they were with, what they did with them and how they felt. All of these factors fall in the realm of *social* and *emotional utilities.*

Functional utility relates to what the product *basically* does. It is a commodity. It is the starting point but it rarely provides significant differentiation. Let's call this the necessary condition. A watch must tell time accurately, a theme park must have rides that are both safe and provide some enjoyment and a fast food restaurant must serve food, fast. Beyond this functionality, what else is provided?

Social and Emotional utilities are more intangible since they deal with feelings and self-beliefs. Often these two utilities are intertwined. When the iPod first came out, Apple was not the preferred name on college campuses. But, as the white iPod buds proliferated, more and more students were swayed by Apple's hipness. This led to a greater penetration of Macs which then begat iPhones and iPads. This virtuous cycle is a good example of social utility.

What do you see in most beer commercials? There is a set of cool people having fun, seemingly living life to the hilt and then there is this one gawky looking fellow on the outside who wants to be cool. Being perceived as cool and socially adept creates social utility. This in turn can make us feel better about ourselves thereby providing a dollop of emotional utility too.

To get a better sense of these utilities, let's try to quantify them by dividing 100 points between the three utilities. *This is not a scientific equation so there are no right answers. Is it arbitrary? Yes. Nevertheless, the exercise will give you insight that is directionally correct.*

This is my best guess for the utilities for Disneyland:

Utility		
Functional:	*20%*	*It provides fun rides*
Social:	*30%*	*It's fun to visit with friends*
Emotional:	*50%*	*Great memories are created*

I think that emotional satisfaction creates the most value at Disneyland. Walt Disney created these theme parks to make people happy and he obviously succeeded. The social value created by being with your family and friends is also significant.

We don't have to agree on our answers. As they say, "Your mileage may vary." This is just an exercise to understand a business in one more way.

What would your allocations be for Walmart? This is what I came up with:

Utility		
Functional:	*90%*	*People go there for the price*
Social:	*0%*	*Nobody brags about it*
Emotional:	*10%*	*Saving money provides some delight*

How about *Nike*? Why are people willing to pay $200, or more, for a pair of sneakers to walk around in? Will you run faster or jump higher? Or is it because it makes you feel that you might just have a bit of LeBron James in you? My guess is:

Utility		
Functional:	*20%*	*The high price is rationalized based on quality, fit and the looks*
Social:	*30%*	*It signals that you are serious about fitness*
Emotional:	*50%*	*"Be like Mike" used to be the song people hummed when Michael Jordan was around. Today it might be "Got Game?"*

These utilities often vary by country and culture. In Brazil, for example, the population is very brand conscious and really likes to dress up. Branded sneakers there cost more than two or three times what we pay in the United States. Nevertheless, they love buying expensive sneakers, even though the greatest wear and tear of these sneakers takes place in shopping malls rather than at the gyms. For Brazil the ratings might be:

Utility	
Functional:	*20%*
Social:	*50%*
Emotional	*30%*

105

Think of other products that have a heavy dollop of emotional utility, e.g. jewelry, purses, perfume, chocolate, perhaps a Rolls Royce? Or is that mainly social utility at play?

By thinking about products and services in this way your understanding of "utility" and the "job hired to do" will increase significantly.

The Utility Equation

A quick recap: Pricing reflects the bundle of value that a customer receives from a product. The marketing utilities - functional, social and emotional - are an excellent way to think about this bundle of value.

At the start of the chapter we asked why are people willing to pay much more for a meal at Chipotle than at McDonald's? At McDonald's, you will get decent food, fairly priced, with efficient service. These all point to the functional utility. Children may still experience emotional and social utilities as they and their friends gulp down a happy meal.

Chipotle's users as noted earlier are environmentally conscious, socially focused and image conscious. Not surprisingly, Chipotle focuses far more on the environmental and social themes than McDonald's. While their customized food might provide higher functional utility, it is their focus on the social and emotional utilities that ultimately lets them charge higher prices.

What do you think makes a Rolex worth $10,000 or more? Let's first think about a Casio. It tells time and it is cheap and it provides significant functional utility. However, it has no social or emotional utility. When was the last time you bragged about owning a Casio?

For Rolex, the functional utility is probably 10-20%. It tells time accurately, it is beautifully made, it will last for a long time and the solid gold structure is handsome and expensive.

The remaining 80-90% utility though, falls in the social and emotional realms. How it is divided between those two utilities can be debated, but a good guess might be 30% social and 50-60% emotional. People buy a Rolex because they can. It allows them to make both a social and emotional statement.

We have developed the following utility equation:

Emotional Utility > *Social Utility* > *Functional Utility*

The highest value is created through emotional utility, followed by social utility, with the functional utility being mostly a commodity. The pricing power follows accordingly. A pair of jeans at Target will be inexpensive because the utility is mostly functional. A pair of designer jeans at Rag & Bone will set you back $250, which is indicative of much greater social and emotional utilities.

As you design your product or service, work towards moving beyond pure functionality. Remember most of the marketing value is created in the social and emotional domains.

Are you still teary eyed thinking about Disneyland? Have a good cry and move on the next chapter. After you the assignment that is.

Assignment: What is the Marketing Utility of your product?

1. What is your product being *hired* to do? (Keep it simple!)

2. Describe in a sentence or two what your product does *for* the customer, especially how it makes them feel?

3. Using 100 points, give your product a score for each of these elements:

    a. Functional utility:

    b. Social utility:

    c. Emotional utility:

    Total: 100

    We believe that the highest pricing is obtained for emotional utility followed by social utility. Functional utility is a commodity. Can you really win on price?

4. Are there ways to enhance the emotional and social utilities of your product? If so, how?

5. **Now do the utility calculation for your competitors:**

Competitors	#1	#2	#3
Functional Utility			
Social Utility			
Emotional Utility			
Total	100	100	100

Does this chart give you any pause for thought? Any actions you need to take?

Additional Notes

Chapter 9

COMPETITION

"The competitor to be feared is one who never bothers about you at all but goes on making his own business better all the time." - Henry Ford

"We look for opportunities where we can offer something better, fresher and more valuable and we seize them. We often move into areas where the customer received a poor deal and where the competition is complacent. And with our growing e-commerce activities, we also look to deliver old products in new ways. We are proactive and quick to act, often leaving bigger and more cumbersome organizations in our wake" - Richard Branson

"If you don't have a competitive advantage, don't compete." - Jack Welch

~~~~~~~~

Key Topics In This Chapter

- Competitive Analysis

    1. Industry Size and Growth

    2. Market Segments

    3. Key Competitors

    4. Opportunities

- Many Ways to Segment

- A Common Mistake

- ASSIGNMENT: Analyze your industry and competitors

Competitive Analysis

To differentiate and position your business you must understand the competitive landscape by focusing on four key elements:

1. *Industry Size and Growth:* How big is the industry and what is its growth rate?
2. *Market Segments:* Every industry can be dissected in a variety of ways into market segments. Each segment focuses on a bundle of value that appeals to a customer. A company has to decide which segment it wants to play in and, if possible, dominate that segment. Walmart is the leader in the price segment in household goods. In the organic food segment, Whole Foods provides leadership. For fast hamburgers, McDonald's excels.
3. *Key Competitors:* You need to understand trends. Who are your key competitors and what are their strengths and weaknesses? Share of market and its change, are a good indicator of the underlying strength of a business.
4. *Opportunities:* Every industry offers possible opportunities. Look for gaps and unmet needs. What advantage are you planning to focus on and why will you succeed?

Research

To collect and evaluate this data requires research. Besides the usual "Googling," there are numerous publications from the Government and Industry Trade Associations that provide relevant data. Market leaders also provide a treasure trove of data with financial reports and analyst presentations. White Papers can often be good sources of information as well. Consulting, venture capital and branding firms often release consumer and industry reports. Many companies also sell data and reports for this very purpose.

You will not suffer from lack of data; rather you'll be inundated by it. Your challenge is to take that vast amount of data and distill it into key, actionable insights. Charts and graphs often tell a better story than pages and pages of statistics and analysis.

A research plan, using the above template, can help you remain organized and focused. Research is like putting a jigsaw puzzle together. The more pieces you fit together, the clearer the picture becomes. Use common sense and make assumptions where necessary. Try to verify the information from more than one source.

An Experiment

I decided to use this approach to look at two industries I wanted to understand better:

1. *Global Media.* What were the major channels, who was gaining market share, what was declining, where was the heart of the action and who was winning?

2. *The U.S. Restaurant Business.* Which segments were gaining ground, what were the key trends and where would future growth most likely come from?

For each industry I spent about 60 minutes collecting data from a variety of sources on the Internet and analyzing it. A composite picture of this analysis is given below. *The purpose of this exercise was to see how much I could learn in a short time. The answer: A lot.* I suspect you will be able to do even better.

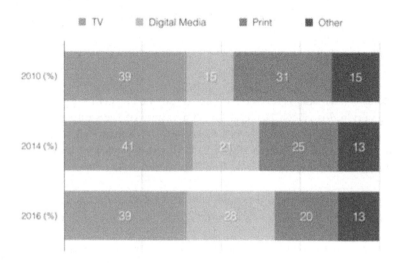

	TV	Digital Media	Print	Other
2010 (%)	39	15	31	15
2014 (%)	41	21	25	13
2016 (%)	39	28	20	13

Global Media

- *Industry Size & Growth*: 2014 worldwide revenues are estimated to be in the $550-580 billion range. The industry is growing at about 6% per year currently.

- *Segments & Trends*:

The trends clearly indicate the explosive growth of digital media with market share increasing from 15% in 2010 to 21% today and expected to be at 28% in 2016. Print media, i.e. newspapers and magazines, have continued to lose share and are forecasted to be only *20% of* total media spending in 2016.

In the United States these trends are even more severe. Total annual spending amounts to $180 billion. Of this amount, digital media accounts for 28% while print is only 18%. Digital is expected to equal TV by 2018. Notably, the fastest growth is coming from mobile media which looks to double to approximately 10%.

- *Key Competitors:* TV and print ownership is diffused generally by country. Digital media, in contrast, is far more global. The two main players are Google and Facebook with 2014 sales of $60 billion and $15 billion respectively.

The mobile segment grew by 75% in 2014[13] and now accounts for nearly one-quarter of all global digital spending. Facebook and Google capture more than two-thirds of such spending. All other companies, including Microsoft and Yahoo, lag well behind.

- *Potential Opportunities:* The greatest opportunities appear to be in digital media especially in the mobile segment. People are spending more time and making more transactions on their smart phones. Ease of use and novelty attract customers. While it is hard to break into this circle of attention, once achieved, the incremental growth costs are low and profitability high.

TV, radio and Outdoor billboards may hold their own for some time, but will see modest erosion. Print media will continue to hemorrhage unless they find a new model or offer unique content as *The Wall Street Journal* and *Financial Times* do.

The best opportunities then lie in engaging the customer at their point of interest, their smartphone for example, in a manner that captivates them. Facebook, Instagram, Snapchat and Pinterest appear to excel here.

---

[13] Source: eMarketer

U.S. Restaurant Industry

- *Industry Size & Growth*: There are 990,000 restaurants with annual sales totaling $683 billion. They employ 13.5 million people, almost one out of every 10 people working. One-half of all adults appear to have worked in this industry sometime in their life and almost a third got their first start working in a restaurant. Growth is only 3%, mostly coming from inflation.

- *Segments:* Total Sales $683 billion

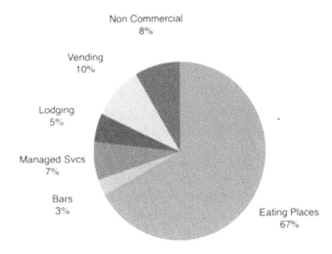

The "Eating Places" can also be further broken down by style of dining. You will recognize most of these names.

	% *	*Top 5*
Casual Dining	32	Applebee's, Olive Garden, Chili's, Buffalo Wild Wings, Outback.
Fast Casual	27	Panera, Chipotle, Five Guys, Qdoba, Einstein Bagels
Quick Service	27	McDonald's, Subway, Starbucks, Burger King, Wendy's
Family Dining	32	IHOP, Denny's, Cracker Barrel, Waffle House, Bob Evans
* % of Restaurant Sales. Some restaurants may appear in more than one segment.		

Some Key Trends:
- Locally sourced products – meat, seafood, produce
  - 64% of the consumers are more likely to visit a restaurant that offers locally produced food items.
Environmental sustainability

- 58% of the consumers are likely to make a restaurant choice based on its environmental sustainability efforts.

Gluten-free

Healthy meals, including meals for kids

- 72% of the consumers are more likely to visit a restaurant that offers healthful options.

Spicy items

Similar trends are also cropping up in the choice of liquor.

- Micro-distilled / artisan spirits.
- Locally produced beer /wine / spirits
- Onsite barrel-aged drinks
- Culinary cocktails
- Regional signature cocktails

- *Key Competitors*[14]: With the data in hand, one can do an extensive competitive analysis. Let's take a look at the "Fast Casual" segment and see what we can learn about three restaurants that we have alluded to in an earlier chapter.

Panera Bread is one of the largest bakery-café chains in the restaurant industry with more than 1,600 U.S. locations and more than $4 billion in U.S. sales. Estimated Sales / Unit: $2.5 million.

Chipotle Mexican Grill is a leader in the fast-casual segment. They are known for their burritos, salads and bowls made with ingredients prepared from sustainable sources, including naturally raised meats and organic and local produce where possible. Sales: $3.19 billion. Total Units: 1,572. Estimated Sales / Unit: $2.1 million.

Qdoba Mexican Grill is a fast-casual restaurant chain with over 600 locations in the U.S. In 2003, the Wheat Ridge, Colorado, based brand was acquired by publicly traded restaurant company Jack in the Box Inc. Sales: $591 million. Total Units: 613. Sales / Unit: $1 million.

- *Potential Opportunities:* There is an interesting dichotomy unfolding in the restaurant arena. On the one hand, there is pressure to keep prices low. People still want inexpensive fast food and continue to be price conscious. On the other hand, there is now an explosive demand for "locally produced foods," "handcrafted beers," and "culinary cocktails" driven by societal trends, increased income in some quarters, and a desire to treat yourself well.

The opportunity, therefore, does not lie on the low end of the restaurant spectrum, but rather in the more specialized segments. Chipotle's focus on environmental factors as well as local produce, humane meats, and custom assembled burritos has developed a strong following. Even in something as basic as hamburgers, Five Guys offers a higher quality, more expensive hamburger than McDonald's to an appreciative audience. Shake Shack, one of fast casual's latest darlings, sells "custard" and "hand cut fries" and had a very lucrative IPO at the end of 2014 with a valuation of $1.6 billion.

In the segment of theme restaurants, you are likely to encounter items that evoke goodness and exotic imagination: locally produced arugula plucked last night, topped with sliced Indian mango, drizzled with sun-drenched olive oil from an undiscovered Greek island. Fusion, imagination and personable service are now integral parts of the new kind of dining experience. This experience is the new opportunity.

---

[14] This data is from Restaurant Association and is for Fiscal 2013.

Many Ways to Segment

As we saw above, the restaurant business has been segmented by service (full, limited) or by style (full, casual, fast casual and quick service).

It is useful to think about several different ways to segment so as to discover new opportunities where unmet needs still exist.

The most basic of these "value adds" are the *price* and *service* levels. A simple example is Walmart. People drive long distances to shop there because of the low prices while accepting an adequate level of service. For more service and a willingness to pay somewhat higher prices, you are likely to turn to a national or local chain nearer your home, perhaps a King Sooper or a Safeway in the Denver area. Close to home, you might stop at an independently owned grocery store where the prices are high but the owner greets you by name.

There is almost a limitless way to segment: price, service, value, demographics, speed, ethnicity, style, etc. A graphic from the April 2015 issue of *Fast Company* details the segmentation of the apparel industry very well. The chart captures the challenge that the retailer Gap finds itself. It is in the middle and needs to make "... clothes that people actually want to wear." Being in the plum center of such a chart is not a good place to be. When you try to please everybody, you end up pleasing very few people.

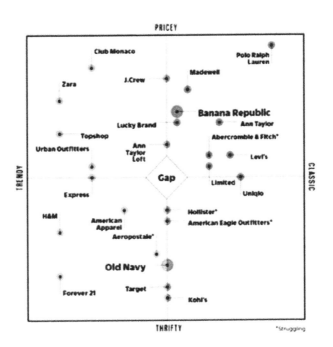

Occasionally, a company can develop advantages on several dimensions. For example, Amazon initially competed with bookstores on price and breadth of selection. They won that war. Then they expanded their offerings and started to offer electronics, for example, at a price better than Best Buy's prices. Even though Best Buy's local presence offered the advantage of convenience, its anemic service made their bundle of value unattractive. They continue to chisel away at the distance disadvantage with their Amazon Prime 2-day service model. Currently it is offering same day service in some markets. Amazon efficiently segments every business it enters. It is the big gorilla in the low price segment with Amazon, but it also offers a full-priced, high service, selection of shoes and clothing through Zappos, a company that it owns.

A Common Mistake

Many people make the mistake of looking at a large category and assuming that they can develop a nice sized business by getting a small share of the market. Their reasoning might go as follows: China has more than a billion people. It seems feasible to reach 2% of the market and sell them four cereal boxes a year at $2 / box. This would allow our business to scale to $160 million rapidly.

Even though the numbers seem small and therefore "conservative", such as only a 2% market share and only four cereal boxes a year, they are based on more hope than reality. The better questions to ask might be:

1. How many people eat cereal in China?
2. How many boxes per year do the cereal eaters buy?
3. Which companies are selling cereals there today? How big are they? What is their experience to date?
4. What will be our point of difference?

Beware of the beguiling fallacy of large numbers.

Assignment: Analyze your Industry and Competitors

Industry

1. What is the size of the industry?

2. What is its growth rate?

3. What are some of the key trends?

-
-
-
- .

4. What are some of the key issues?

-
-
-

Competitive Landscape

Competitors	#1	#2	#3	YOU
Products				
Price Points				
Customers				
Point of Difference				
Strength of management				
Strength of marketing efforts				
Strength of sales efforts				

Now develop a segmentation map for your industry? What are the key dimensions that should be on the axes?

Segmentation Map

Are you satisfied by your positioning? Do you have a true competitive advantage?

Napoleon said, "If you start to take Vienna, take Vienna." It's time to take Vienna!

Additional Notes

Chapter 10

VISUALIZING THE CUSTOMER

"We see our customers as invited guests to a party, and we are the hosts. It's our job every day to make every important aspect of the customer experience a little bit better." - Jeff Bezos

"Visualizations act as a campfire around which we gather to tell stories." - Al Shalloway

"The greatest value of a picture is when it forces us to notice what we never expected to see." - John Tukey

~~~~~~~~

Key Topics in this Chapter

- Basics: Demographics, Psychographics and Marketing Utility

- Beachhead Target

- Persona

- Assignment: Visualize Your Customer

The two pillars of any business are its customers and its people. While having the right people is crucial to your success, everything starts with your customers.

"There is only one boss. The customer. And he can fire everybody in the company from the chairman on down, simply by spending his money somewhere else." – Sam Walton

It is therefore important that you understand the customer from all angles. Who are they (demographics)? How do they think (psychographics)? What do they value (marketing utility)? Given limited resources, a new business must first focus on its most likely customers, who are called the beachhead target. It is helpful to develop a persona for this prototypical customer. The clearer you can visualize this person, the better you can understand what he needs and why he will buy your product. Please your customer and smile all the way to the bank is a maxim worth remembering.

Basics: Demographics, Psychographics, Marketing Utility

We have touched on these elements earlier. In this section we will put everything together. Feel free to add or subtract from the list to customize it for your customer.

Key Demographics

- Age
- Gender
- Occupation
- Income
- Education
- Ethnicity
- Marital Status
- Children
- College Educated
- Geographic Location

Key Psychographics

- Environmental Focus
- Lifestyle (Active, Sedentary etc.)
- Social Focus (high, medium, low)
- Tech Savvy (high, medium, low)
- Image Conscious
- Financial Focus
- Key beliefs
- What is most important to them?
- What do they fear most?
- What do they read?
- Where do they travel?
- What shows do they like?

Marketing Utility

Divide the Marketing Utility pie of 100 points into the three utilities, Functional, Social and Emotional. In one sentence explain what you believe your customer is seeking from your product.

Two Examples

With Professor Dobie's help we have developed this data for Chipotle (which was shared in an earlier chapter) and Apple.

Chipotle

Demographics:
- 60% Female, 40% Male
- Age 18-34
- Income of $10-60K per year
- 82% Caucasian
- 44% College Educated
- 69% Have no children

Psychographics:
- Environmentally conscious
- Active lifestyle
- Socially focused
- Tech savvy
- Image conscious
- Financially focused

Utility:
- 60% Functional
- 30% Social
- 10% Emotional

Apple

Demographics
- Age 18-34
- Urban dwellers
- Middle/upper income ($100K)
- 67% have college degree
- Strong verbal aptitude

Psychographics:
- Lifestyle focus
- 58% consider themselves "liberal" in politics
- Early adopter of new technology

- Want to be perceived as unique and different
- Appreciate simplicity and want to remove complexity from lives
- Prefer modern art and are design enthusiasts
- Throw more parties
- Care about the way the brand connects on a human level
- Less modest than PC users
- More assured of their own superiority

Utility:
- 30% Functional
- 50% Social
- 20% Emotional

Beachhead Target

Too many companies try to appeal to a broad base of customers and try to meet a large sets of requirements. However, they end up diluting their product, their connection with the customer, and overstretching their own abilities. The results are rarely satisfactory. One of the great axioms of life is that *you cannot be everything to everybody*. Another good rule of thumb is the Pareto Principle which states that 80% of the value is created by 20% of the customers.

You must focus on those customers that really want your product and who you have the ability to serve exceptionally well. It means making choices, doing fewer things and keeping a sharp focus. It requires developing a beachhead target of customers that you will *start with*. You will live and die with them at this stage.

What then are some of the key characteristics of this beachhead group? In *Disciplined Entrepreneurship*, Bill Aulet[15] suggests seven criteria, which we have paraphrased as follows:

1. Can the target afford your product?
2. Do they have a compelling reason to buy your product?
3. Can you deliver the product to them through your channels?
4. Can you deliver a complete product?
5. Can you overcome any existing competition to deliver your product?
6. Will this segment open doors to other segments?
7. Is this target consistent with your passions and values?

This is a variation of the questions that you have already been thinking about. Now is a good time to look at these questions afresh and answer them.

Different kinds of people adopt new products at different times. There are people who are always trying new things ("early adopters") and then there are people who are a century or two behind ("laggards"). The chart below, which appears in most marketing textbooks, gives you an idea of these different sets of people and their rate of adoption.

---

[15] Aulet, Bill. *Disciplined Entrepreneurship*. Hoboken, NJ: John Wiley & Sons, Inc., 2013

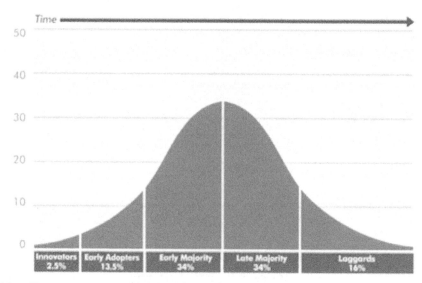

The "Beachhead" customers are most often found amongst the innovators and early adopters.

Developing a Persona

By now you have collected a lot of information about your target customer. In *Disciplined Entrepreneurship* the author suggests developing a *"Persona"* for your customer. Who is your customer as a person? Can you articulate a persona for this person given all the details that you have developed? Go further and develop a picture or a sketch of this person.

Sometimes this person might be on your team, especially if the product is a passion for one of you. At other times, it might be someone who you know well or a customer you have come across in the past. It can also be a composite picture of various people.

My guess is, that if you took "selfies" of yourself or a friend, many of you would be looking at the Chipotle and Apple personas.

Developing a Persona is a powerful tool. It will guide you in your decision making, because now you will have a clear image of the customer you are trying to appeal to.

Assignment: Visualize Your Customer

Now it is time for you to visualize your customer. The clearer the image of your customer in your mind, the better you will understand him.

Key Demographics of Your Customer

Describe your customer in a sentence or two for each of these elements. The more detail the better:

Age Range:

Gender:

Occupation:

Income:

Education:

Ethnicity:

Marital Status:

Children:

College Educated:

Geographic Location:

Other Demographics:

Key Psychographics

Environmental Focus:

Lifestyle (Active, Sedentary etc.):

Social Focus (high, medium, low):

Tech Savvy (high, medium, low):

Image Conscious:

Financial Focus:

Key beliefs:

What is most important to them?

What do they fear most?

What do they read?

Where do they travel?

What shows do they like?

Marketing Utility

Divide the Marketing Utility pie of 100 points into the three utilities: Functional, Social and Emotional.

Type	Number of Points
Functional	_____
Social	_____
Emotional	_____
Total	**100**

In one sentence explain what you believe your customer is seeking from your product.

Persona

Do you now have a good image of who your customer is? Articulate a **Persona** for your customer: Write a paragraph describing this person.

Now draw a **picture** of your customer. Perhaps this person is someone on your team, or someone who you know, or maybe it is a composite picture of various people. Whatever the case may be, unleash your artistic talent and create a picture of your customer.

"Visualizations act as a campfire around which we gather to tell stories." - Al Shalloway

Additional Notes

Chapter 11

CHANNELS OF DISTRIBUTION

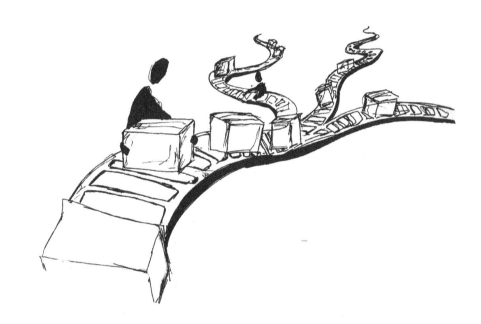

"Today's leading real-world retailer, Walmart, uses software to power its logistics and distribution capabilities, which it has used to crush its competition." - Marc Andreessen

"Distribution has really changed. You can make a record with a laptop in the morning and have it up on YouTube in the afternoon and be a star overnight." - Bonnie Raitt

"To go indie is a thing. But to put an album in the stores, you need a distribution label." - Drake

~~~~~~~~

Key Topics in this Chapter

- Direct Channels of Distribution

- Indirect Channels of Distribution

- Cost of Complexity

- Using Multiple Channels

- Assignment: How will you distribute your products?

You have developed a clearer idea of your industry and your potential competitors. It is now time to determine how you will get your product to your customer and what channels of distribution you will use. There are two main ways in which companies distribute products to customers - direct and indirect.

Direct Channels of Distribution

In the direct channel, a company sells directly to the customer without an intermediary.

Direct

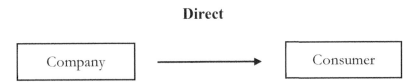

There are many examples of direct channel distribution such as:

- *Web*: Customers buy directly from the website and the product is shipped to them. Examples include Amazon, Apple, virtually all retailers and a host of other companies.
- *Web downloads*: This is even better and faster. Customers buy and download software, music or movies immediately. iTunes, Microsoft and most software companies offer this option.
- *Retail locations*: This is the predominant channel for most businesses, including:
    - o All restaurants: Chipotle, McDonald's, KFC, Olive Garden and every coffee shop you have ever been to including Starbucks, Peet's Coffee and Dunkin Donuts.
    - o All retailers: Best Buy, Macy's, grocery stores, office supply stores, hardware stores, etc.
    - o Many services: Doctors, hairdressers, dry cleaners and financial advisors.
- *Store pickup*: Domino's and Ikea are prominent examples.
- *Home delivery*: Pizza places
- *Home care*: Lawn care, plumbers, electricians and most trade services.
- *Farmer's markets*
- *Home shopping TV channels*
- *Infomercials*
- *Catalogs*
- *Vending machines*

Indirect Channels of Distribution

In this case intermediaries are utilized to deliver the products to the customers.

Indirect

Company	·····▶	Retailer	·····▶	Consumer
Company	····▶	Wholesaler	····▶ Retailer	····▶ Consumer
Company	··▶ Agent	··▶ Wholesaler	··▶ Retailer	··▶ Consumer

The retailer is the key gatekeeper in this form of distribution. The retailer does not generally make the product. Rather companies sell their products to retailers who then sell it to customers. Both the manufacturer and the retailer see the customers as their customers.

- *Company - Retailer - Consumer*
    - P&G sells Crest, Tide and Gillette to Walmart who then sells it to us.
    - Publishers like Random House and Hatchette sell books to Amazon, which in turn sells them to you and me.

- *Company - Wholesaler - Retailer - Consumer*
    - A retail location can rarely hold a truckload of any one product whether it's toothpaste, cereal or detergent. In such cases, manufacturers sell their products to wholesalers, who have the capacity to hold large inventories. Retailers then order a *combination* of products from these wholesalers in truckload quantities. These products are then stocked in the retail stores where consumers can buy them.
    - Let's follow the story of a box of *Cap'n Crunch* from its birth to its consumption in your house. The cereal is manufactured at a Quaker Oats' plant and then shipped to a wholesaler. A retailer like Jewel in Chicago or Vons in Los Angeles will then order a variety of products to fill a truck from such a wholesaler. The truck brings the assortment of the products to the local stores. You then go in and buy a box of Cap'n Crunch and take it home or eat it eagerly on the way back.

- *Company - Agent - Wholesaler - Retailer - Consumer*
    - Sometimes another step is involved in the distribution process. Specialty products that are smaller in scale will hire an agent to represent them in dealing with the retail trade. Such agents represent many small companies, have marketing and retail expertise and help these smaller companies get distribution and product movement. Most stores will have a specialty aisle for such items. If a product is successful, it will often be bought out by a larger company. Vitamin Water, Odwalla and Naked Juice are examples of this phenomenon.

Cost of Complexity

Not surprisingly, the more hands or "touches" that are required in the distribution channel, the greater the costs of distribution become. A retailer, wholesaler or an agent all add to the cost structure.

There are two main reasons that Walmart is the low cost leader. The first is that its scale allows it to negotiate better prices from vendors. The second reason is that they have optimized their supply chain by examining all aspects of the distribution system and eliminating all unnecessary steps, i.e. "touches." This allows them to carry lower inventory for shorter periods of time. Both sets of cost savings are then passed on to customers in the form of lower prices.

Let's look at the Cap'n Crunch example again. Quaker Oats sells a truckload of the cereal to Walmart, which takes delivery of the cereal in its own warehouses and quickly, often within 24 hours, distributes it along with other products to fill a truck, to their own stores. You then buy it from their store.

Contrary to popular belief, most companies like dealing with Walmart because their efficient system is less aggravating. It also allows both Walmart and the producing company to make more money and the customer to benefit from lower prices.

Complexity has a cost. This is why selling directly through the web is simple, efficient and cost effective. All you need is an excellent website and an account with FedEx, UPS and USPS to do a good job.

Using Multiple Channels

A distribution channel allows you to sell to a customer. When you start a business, you may have only one channel, but when it becomes cost effective, you may expand to multiple channels. Below are some well-known examples to give you ideas for your business:

- Domino's Pizza has two channels – delivery and pick up from the store.
- Apple has three channels– their website, the Apple stores and other retailers such as Amazon and Best Buy.
- The Apple stores have been a rousing success. Not only do they allow the company to sell the product, they more importantly set a tone and relationship with the customer that is crucial. Dell and Gateway, companies that made PCs some years ago, failed in this channel. It will be interesting to see how the Microsoft stores fare. Will they be able to develop a relationship with the customer as Apple has?
- Walmart sells primarily through its stores, but is making a huge effort to expand into e-commerce.
- Amazon's key channel is its website. They recently announced they would open a retail store in New York.
- Starbucks' primary channel is its coffee shops, but they also sell through grocery stores and Amazon.
- Warby Parker started online, but ended 2014 with 10 retail stores. They plan to double this by year-end 2015.
- A consulting company is likely to have two channels. Its primary distribution channel will most likely be on-site visits while its secondary channel may include online delivery of content, Skype, or phone conversations.

Expanding distribution channels does allow more points of interaction, but it is expensive. Brick and mortar retail stores are far more expensive than a website. Furthermore, each channel requires additional expertise. Caution is advised when expanding channels.

What does this mean for you? For the starting entrepreneur, costs are a big issue. Start with a channel where you can get the most bang for your buck. You can always add more channels later.

Assignment: How will you distribute your products?

Keep it simple. Stay within your means. It generally makes sense to start with one channel.

What channel will you initially focus on?

What are the key things you will need to get started in this channel?

What will you need to get started if you are going to sell from your website?

If you want to sell through Whole Foods (or some other retailer), how will you convince them to give you a trial?

o   Are there distributors that can help you with this? Have you talked to them?

Are you thinking of a home service of some kind? Which geographical area will you start with?

o   How many people will you need?

You get the idea. Pick one channel to start with and get started.

Additional Notes

Chapter 12

POSITIONING, BRAND, PRICING & PROMOTION

"In this ever-changing society, the most powerful and enduring brands are built from the heart. They are real and sustainable. Their foundations are stronger because they are built with the strength of the human spirit, not an ad campaign. The companies that are lasting are those that are authentic." - Howard Schultz

"The first lesson of branding: memorability. It's very difficult buying something you can't remember." - John Hegarty

"Brand and product don't compete. Brand is product, and everything else conforming to the unique story that consumers create when they think of you." - Laura Busche

~~~~~~~~

Key Topics in this Chapter

- Positioning

- Brand

- Pricing

- Promotion

- Assignment: Develop positioning, brand, pricing and a promotional plan for your business.

Positioning

You have learned that industries can be segmented in many ways. The combination of these attributes creates a bundle of value that positions the product.

In *Breakthrough Branding*, Catherine Kaputo[16] offers the following definition of *Positioning*: "a clear benefit or promise of worth that your product can own in the minds of prospects and (one) that is different from that of its competitors."

Kaputo believes that there are two big motivators in branding:

1. An appeal to *benefits and consequences* such as going to McDonald's and being confident that you will get the same thing every time.
2. An appeal to the *emotions* and *desires* of people to belong to a certain group or set of ideas, which then becomes an *identity*. Have you ever been passionate about a sports team? Have you ever donned your favorite band's t-shirt and felt like you were part of something bigger? If yes, then you've already started crafting your own identity.

Ms. Kaputo offers several possible positioning strategies. I have picked five of these to focus on. You may want to read her excellent book and view the entire list and learn much more about marketing.

1. *"Own an Attribute* – (such a) positioning appeals to the left side of the brain, the rational side that wants clear-cut distinctions about brand benefits and characteristics. For years, Verizon Wireless positioned the brand around having a superior cell signal with its "Test Man" and its breakthrough "Can You Hear Me Now?" advertising campaign. Having a better cell signal was a great attribute to own because it meant more reliable service.
2. *"Target a Specific Group* - Look at the old "I'm a Mac and you're a PC" campaign. Who do you identity with? The hip Mac guy or the conservative PC guy? The Mac guy appears on the right and is much younger and dressed in jeans. The PC guy wears nerdy glasses, ill-fitting khakis and a jacket and tie. The campaign appeals to people who aspire to hipness and it helped propel Apple's share of the computer market, attracting large numbers of former PC owners to make the switch.
3. *"Be the First* - Being the first in a category is powerful… Jeff Bezos created the first online retail bookstore. It is still number one and has expanded successfully beyond books.
4. *"Be the Leader* - Bill Gates set out to be the leader in computing with this mission: 'A computer on every desk and in every home, all running Microsoft software.' It was a breakthrough branding statement for computing in 1975…when few people had a computer or could even imagine using one in their personal lives.
5. *"Align with a Cause* - Look at TOMS Shoes: for every pair of its iconic cloth, rubber-soled "alpargatas" shoes sold, TOMS Shoes gives away a pair to someone who needs it."

Some of the other possibilities include positioning as a maverick (Apple originally, but not now), having a special ingredient (Stevia in Truvia), connecting with a celebrity (Nike and Michael Jordan) and being the low cost leader (Walmart or even Amazon). While some of these examples are not recent, they do explain the concepts well.

Professor Gretchen Dobie believes that a positioning statement must define the following three components:

1. Who is your target customer?

---

[16] Kaputo, Catherine. *Breakthrough Branding*. Boston: Nicholas Brealey, 2012.

2. What is your product?
3. Why should your target customer buy your "competitive advantage," meaning your "point of difference?"

Let's look at a few positioning statements. For *Quaker Oatmeal Squares*, Professor Dobie suggests the following:

> To Female Heads of Household seeking a wholesome breakfast *(Target Market)*, Quaker Oatmeal Squares is the *only* wholesome ready-to-eat cereal *(The Product)* that offers all the traditional benefits you associate with the Quaker Man *(Point of Difference)*.

While studying IKEA in class we arrived at the following positioning statement:

> To cost conscious young adults looking to buy furniture *(Target Market)*, Ikea offers inexpensive, good quality, stylish, contemporary, ready-to-assemble furniture *(The Product)*, sold in an engaging, fun and attractive setting *(Point of Difference)*.

In another class we studied the case[17] of a French cookie company *Michel et Augustin* which developed the following positioning statement:

> "For young adults who want a sweet indulgent snack *(Target Market)*, Michel et Augustin is a brand of sablé cookies in small packages that provide a tasty snack *(The Product)* and the invitation to be part of an authentic gourmet adventure unlike everything you know because they are made with natural ingredients by Michel and Augustin, childhood friends with a mission to make the world smile *(Point of Difference)*."

The last positioning statement is a bit wordier (it is French after all) than we would recommend, but it captures the "bundle of value" of the brand. Don't you want to eat the cookie right now and join the adventure?

Brand

A product is generic - carrots, computers, phones. A brand gives the product an identity, a personality, an emotional connection, or even a call to action.

Amazon CEO, Jeff Bezos: *"A brand for a company is like a reputation for a person. You earn reputation by trying to do hard things well."*

Designer, Tommy Hilfiger: *"I knew exactly what I wanted to do. I wanted to build some kind of lifestyle brand that was preppy and cool."*

Actress, Katherine Hepburn: *"My greatest strength is common sense. I'm really a standard brand - like Campbell's tomato soup or Baker's chocolate."*

What emotion do you feel when you see Disney's Mickey Mouse symbol? Do thoughts of childhood, good times or an especially memorable trip come to mind? That is what a great brand does. Here are some more examples:

---

[17] INSEAD: Michel et Augustin Cookies: Culinary Adventurers Competing Against Food Industry Giants

- The brand name Quaker Oats was created to evoke the simple, true values of the Quaker people.
- *ESPN* today connotes sports, action, something happening, movement, 24/7.
- Apple has evolved from being a maverick, to a stylish, elegant, easy to use eco-system with just a hint of exclusivity.
- Brands can also be tied to a personality such as Rachael Ray and Emeril LaGasse in cooking and Richard Branson in just about all *Virgin* products.
- Over time some brands can become synonymous with a category - for example Kleenex and Xerox and perhaps now even Google.

According to Professor Dobie, the cardinal rule to branding is to be *different* and *memorable*.

A brand must also look and feel the same way everywhere, in every medium. Branding encompasses positioning, packaging, a name and pricing.

Some rules of thumb for a good brand name are:

- Short (IBM, BMW)
- Distinct (Google, Yahoo, Mustang)
- Sounds good (Zara, Virgin, Disney)
- Suggests a compelling benefit or feature (Facebook, Home Depot, Sunkist Oranges, Spic N' Span cleaner)
- Breaks the rules (Red Bull)
- Easy to say, to spell and recall (Tide soap, Crest toothpaste)
- But make sure that the name does not mean something bad in another language. (The classic case is the introduction of the *Chevy Nova* in South America. Nova means "it doesn't go." Oops.)

A *tagline* to the brand will at times become an integral part of the brand. Sometimes it explains the benefit and at other times it captures the image of the brand memorably. Some of the most memorable taglines according to a *Forbes*[18] article are:

1. *BMW*: Ultimate Driving Machine
2. *Nike*: Just Do It
3. *American Express*: Don't Leave Home Without It
4. *Avis*: We Try Harder
5. *California Milk Processor Board*: Got Milk?
6. *Apple:* Think Different
7. *U.S. Marines:* The Few. The Proud. The Marines
8. *McDonald's:* You Deserve A Break Today
9. *DeBeers:* A Diamond Is Forever
10. *MasterCard:* There Are Some Things Money Can't Buy. For Everything Else, There's MasterCard

These are indeed memorable taglines. They capture the benefits and even more importantly the emotional and social benefits of the brands extraordinarily well. Many years ago, when people found out that I was President of the company that owned *Rice-A-Roni*, they would joyously break out into song: "Rice-A-Roni, the San Francisco Treat." Those memories still make me smile. Talk about a tagline.

Finally, you must execute all the elements consistently. Apple does this extraordinarily well. Their products are stylish and appear to work seamlessly together. The packaging has the same feel: sophisticated and understated, providing confidence that everything will just work. Apple's website is clean and makes it easy to find what you are looking for. Their stylish stores, with the open glass look, both welcome a person and make it easy for them to buy something. Every channel delivers the same consistent message.

---

[18] *Forbes*: May 2010: "Best-Loved Advertising Taglines"

Pricing

How should you price your product or service? It is normal for entrepreneurs to want to price low to try and get sales to get started. This is understandable and sometimes the best approach at the start. However, you must focus on what the ongoing sustainable price will be.

You have done a lot of research to date. You should have a good idea of your target customer, the problem you are solving, the competitive landscape, the marketing utility you are providing and your "point of difference."

These are the key components of pricing. While being competitive, do not underestimate the value you are creating. Why are the prices at Whole Foods higher than at other supermarkets? It is because they are perceived to provide premium, higher quality products that satisfy the functional, social, and emotional utilities of their customers better than the competition. Would lower prices lead to more sales? In the short run perhaps, but in the long run it would diminish the value of the brand.

Why is a Mac priced higher than a PC? A Rolex buyer does not want to buy the $100 Rolex that can be found on the streets of New York. They want something different – the "real thing," the one that gives them an excellent product, social standing and a feeling of "I have made it."

You should experiment with pricing. But always remember: a low price is rarely the right answer. Only one business - Walmart, McDonald's, Amazon - can be the low price leader in a category. Find ways to increase value and then price to reflect this higher value.

Promotional Plan

It's time to turn your attention to how you will communicate with your customers. Promotion embodies both personal and non-personal interactions.

Let's examine the myriad possibilities moving from the micro to the macro. At the outset you may have a very small budget and may have to start with digital media only. As the business grows and the marketing budget increases, you will be able to utilize other media.

Electronic Media

Website	Podcast	Webinars
E-mail Blasts	Blogs	Mobile
Video	Facebook	Twitter
Banner Ads	Social Networks	

Mini Media

Brochures	Public Relations	Yellow Pages
Free Seminars	Free Consultations	Mobile
Free Newsletters	T-Shirts, Pens, Giveaways	Signs/ Banners
Coupons	Rebates	

146

Personal Selling

Sales force	Hire an Agent	Dealers
Distributors	Telemarketing	Trade Shows

Large Media advertising

TV	Newspapers	Radio
Magazines	Outdoor Signs	Direct Mail

As you move from micro to macro media the costs increase rapidly, as does the reach. However, be sure to focus on effectiveness. While a Super Bowl ad might do wonders for your ego and social standing, it may not be the most cost effective use of your money. Always focus on what will work with connecting you and your message to your customer.

Small entrepreneurs are better off starting with social media, free promotions and in-person sales calling. Creativity will be a key ingredient of your success as will persistence and resilience. You will be your best marketing program and sales agent.

Sarah Levy, a friend and frequent guest speaker in my classes, has a love for baking and started her business "Sarah's Candies" in her mom's kitchen. She called on many nearby stores but her big breakthrough came when a buyer at Whole Foods decided to try her cookies in a few stores. The rest is, as they say, history. Luck, for some reason, seems to favor those with initiative and a willingness to work hard.

"I am a great believer in luck, and I find the harder I work, the more I have of it." - Thomas Jefferson

The greatest and purest form of marketing is *word of mouth: nothing beats somebody raving about your product and telling others about it. This is called a referral.* Word of mouth marketing and the power of customer loyalty is a powerful tool that successful brands use. Companies like Disney, Intuit, American Express and Microsoft use a metric called the Net Promoter Score (NPS) to measure how likely a customer is to recommend a firm or a service to a friend. Higher customer loyalty translates into a higher score which augurs well for the growth prospects of the business. Companies like Zappos and Warby Parker insure high NPS by focusing on excellent customer service as a way to build brand identity and drive growth. Focus on figuring out how to get referrals. In today's social media, *going viral is the ultimate referral.*

Assignment: Develop positioning, brand, pricing and promotional plans for your business

This is the most important assignment related to connecting with your customer. Spend the time to do this right.

Positioning

What will be the positioning of your brand?

Why?

Can it really own that position?

Your Positioning Statement

For _____ (target customer), _____ (name of product or

service) is _____(description of product or service), that _____

_____ (point of difference).

Brand Name

What is your brand name?

How did you decide on it?

How is it different and memorable?

Tagline

Brainstorm 5 taglines for your product or service.

1.

2.

3.

4.

5.

Which one did you pick? Why?

Pricing

What is your pricing?

How does it compare to the competition?

What is your rationale for this pricing?

Promotion

Write down the promotional channels you intend to start with.

How can you get word of mouth referrals?

What can you do to "go viral?"

"You have to think of your brand as a kind of myth…. It has to have emotional content and all the themes of a great story: mystery, magic, adventure, intrigue, conflicts, contradiction, paradox." – Deepak Chopra

Additional Notes

Chapter 13

THE ART OF SELLING

"If you don't believe in what you're selling, neither will your prospect." - Frank Bettger

"Create something, sell it, make it better, sell it some more and then create something that obsoletes what you used to make." - Guy Kawasaki

"Mastering the art of selling involves mastering the craft of providing your clients the education, products, services, and personal contact before, during and after the sale that they want, need and, more important, deserve. That's how you succeed. That's how you'll not only survive and grow in this business, but will thrive, prosper, and achieve greatness through it." - Tom Hopkins, How to Master the Art of Selling

~~~~~~~~

Key Topics in this Chapter

- The Art of Selling

- A Sales case study from class

- Assignment: Develop a Selling Strategy for Your Business

Good marketing, it has been said, can make selling obsolete. Apple is an excellent example of this phenomenon. When you get to an Apple store, you don't have to be sold much. You have already sold yourself, but even Apple has to do some selling. First, it has to convince you to go to the store and then subtly sell you when you are there.

Beyond the selling that is required to attract customers, you should also develop personal selling skills. You will need these in many situations, including persuading your teammates to join you, getting potential customers to give you a try, convincing suppliers to ship you raw material and cajoling investors to put up money.

"Everyone lives by selling something." – Robert Louis Stevenson

The Art of Selling

If selling is an essential part of life, why is it that so many of us are afraid to sell? Are you afraid to sell? The fear of failure and being rejected undoubtedly plays a part.

Many people's distaste may also come from having been sold something they did not want. The memory of having bought a used car from an old style car dealership may still haunt you. At that dealership, you were exhausted standing in the burning sun on a Saturday afternoon, sweating in your clothes on the hot pavement and most likely arguing with a particularly persistent car salesman in a polyester suit. You can remember the haggling, with a gnawing certainty, that you were not getting a square deal. The salesperson knew he would never see you again and you just wanted to get it over with and run.

This is called transactional selling and can often leave a bad taste.

Zig Ziglar suggests a different approach to selling. *"How should you prospect? Display a genuine interest in the other person."* Let us call this *relational* selling. As the name implies, this philosophy entails developing a relationship. Some of its key elements are:

1. *Relationships* are the key to life. Emotional Intelligence - meaning how you deal with people - trumps IQ every single time. Even 10 minutes can appear like eternity if you decide to connect with another person on a human level. In our modern milieu, overrun by social media, we mistake casual interaction for relationships. If anything, there is an even greater need for relationships today because of the overwhelming superficiality. Time and time again, my experience has shown me that people yearn for a meaningful conversation, a deeper connection than the ubiquitous "hey."

   Rich Cardillo is one of the best sales and people's person I have ever met. When he took over the Colorado sales operations for a large company, one of his first calls was on an irate client. As he entered the room, he noticed pictures of fish and fishing everywhere. Rich, being an avid fisherman himself, found the perfect conversation icebreaker. Yes, the problem was addressed, but it was the personal connection that cemented the relationship. Twenty years later Rich and that client, now retired, still go fishing together every year.

   Does the story sound far-fetched? Try it. You will be surprised. Listen to the customer of course, fix the problem quickly, but go further. What if you made all encounters an effort in human understanding rather than an exercise trying to figure out "What can I get out of this as quickly as possible?"

   What kind of approach would you like someone to take with you?

2. *Never lie.* It is a sign of the times that we even have to say this. Sometimes people think that small lies are okay. However, invariably small lies become bigger lies and then more lies are needed to support the previous ones. Always put yourselves in the buyer's shoes. Would you rather deal with people that you cannot trust or with those who are honest and upfront?

3. *Know your proposition cold.* What does this mean? Very simply, know your business, know your costs, know what you need to achieve and therefore what you can and cannot do. Let's assume that you really need the

order. Be sure to know the lowest price you can make this work. What if the customer wants a large quantity quickly? Before you say yes, be certain that you can deliver both the quantity and meet the timeline. This is what it means to know your proposition cold. Commit to what you can do and will do. No more, no less.

4. *Know your customer's business cold.* Yes, it is your job to know your customer's business really well, especially if the customer is a buyer for a large organization. He may have responsibility for many products and may not have detailed knowledge about your product category. Understand your customer's business better than he does. You should become the category expert that the customer turns to whenever he has questions or is seeking new ideas.

5. *Start with the customer's needs and not your needs.* Many companies do not approach it this way. This opens up greater opportunity for you as you embrace a "customer centric" approach.

6. *Great sales people also:*
   - Rarely complain
   - Keep perfect records
   - Understand and solve the customer's problems
   - Keep their word

This is the essence of the Art of Selling.

Chet Holmes[19] says something similar in his masterful book *Ultimate Sales Machine:*

1. *Establish rapport.* Everything starts with this. People do business with people they like.

2. *Find the need.* Ask them about their problems and in that conversation the need will appear.

3. *Build value.* Understand the customer's need and problem and then figure out how to solve it. This is how value is built. A lower price can work sometimes, but it is rarely a sustainable value.

4. *Create desire.* By using the right market data and analysis, a customer - especially if the buyer is a large organization - can become highly motivated. Show them where they are losing customers and how your product or service will help them retain existing customers and get more customers. Give them examples of where this has worked before and the impact it has had on the other customers. Show them how this will increase their bottom line.

5. *Overcome objections.* Customers will, and should, have questions and uncertainties. That is your time to shine. Your job is to help them see how your product will meet their needs. Every objection answered makes the sale more likely. We assume, of course, that your product can *actually* do what you are saying. As stated earlier, never lie or overstate. Always under-promise and over-deliver.

6. *Close the sale.* Sometimes all it takes is to shut up. When the customer says he wants to buy your product, say thank you *and shut up.*

7. *Follow up.* Always follow up a meeting with a note of thanks and also be sure to do whatever you committed to doing in the meeting.

---

[19] Holmes, Chet. *Ultimate Sales Machine.* New York: Penguin Group, 2007.

These steps sound so elementary and they are. The good news is that very few people follow them. By making this your modus operandi, you will already be head and shoulders above much of your competition.

Bottom line: think of customer interaction as not a transaction, but a relationship. Instead of focusing on only making a one-time sale, ask yourself how the relationship can be made long lasting. Carl Sewell[20] became one of the biggest and most successful car dealers in the United States. He shared his philosophy in his classic book: *Customers for Life: How to turn that one-time buyer into a lifetime customer*. The title says it all.

A Sales Case Study from Class

Most of the points made above come into sharp focus when we discuss a Harvard Business case[21] in class involving an entrepreneur whose business is struggling because it cannot generate enough sales. With diligence and a bit of luck, he has managed to get an appointment with a large retailer. An order from this retailer could mean the difference between great success and shutting the business down. The stakes in this meeting are high.

The students, in preparing for the class, are urged to understand the "proposition." What can or can't they do to understand the customer's needs in order to make a compelling pitch? Their 10-minute meeting and presentation to the buyer will *make or break the company*.

As part of the homework the night before, every team had to answer a few questions. Most teams indicated a clear understanding of the case and developed a good pitch for the buyer. However, in class an entirely different story unfolds.

I choose three teams randomly to make the sales pitch to a rather cantankerous buyer, played by a friend of mine who is both a professor and a litigation lawyer. The teams come in one by one and the drama begins. Over the years about 80% of the teams have *not* been able to get the order and hence would have gone out of business. Why is this so? These are smart students, articulate, with a capacity to connect with people. Their homework indicates they know everything needed to make the sale. Let's take a look at where the process breaks down.

1. The presenting team students walk in to class full of joie de vivre. They are confident and are looking forward to being successful in front of their classmates.

   Unfortunately, a shock awaits them. The buyer does not remember having an appointment with them. He does not know their product, seems to be short of time and is preoccupied. He is not sure he wants to talk to them. Does this happen in real life? You better believe it. It has happened to me more than once, even when I was running large and well-known companies.

   These students are accustomed to being able to smooth talk their way through most things on campus. They are not prepared for this kind of reception. They get rattled.

2. Feeling the pressure of limited time, they immediately launch into the features and benefits of their product. They make no attempt to connect with the buyer or try to find the buyer's "pain."

3. The good news is their product is compact, needs less shelf space, is attractively packaged and competitively priced. It should make the retailer more money. Nonetheless, the students often forget to tell this to the buyer.

4. The variable cost of the product is $9.50 and generally the teams propose a selling price of $12.50 to the retailer. When the buyer offers to test out their product at $10, which would still allow them to make a small profit and, importantly, get their foot in the door, the teams often forget their math. They dig in their heels and start to negotiate forgetting that the power at present lies with the buyer. Many teams turn down the offer even though such an action will result in going out of business.

---

[20] Sewell, Carl. *Customers for Life*. New York: Doubleday Business, 1990.
[21] Deaver Brown and Cross River Inc., HBR

5. Sometimes the buyer will ask them details about their product. Teams have been known to offer glib answers and to prevaricate.

6. The remainder of students, as observers, enjoy the spectacle. From the safety of the bleachers, they of course think that they would have done much better. One year, an observing team begged me to give them a chance to let them make a sale. They were sure they would "nail" it. So I did. They did not make the sale and fell into the same traps their peers had.

7. So which students get the order? The ones that start with developing a relationship. When the buyer is a bit brusque, they smile. They wait for him to finish what he is doing. They find a way to strike a conversation. They have realized that 10 minutes is plenty of time. They listen. They answer. They are truthful and they know their own and the customer's proposition cold.

They are guided by the mantra: *It's about the customer.* It is not about them. They have embraced the real art of selling. When I see students in later years, many tell me that *this* is the class that they most vividly remember and learned from.

Assignment: A Selling Strategy Template

Fill out this worksheet before every sales call. It will help you get ready!

Who is the customer on *this* call?	
What price will you sell at?	
What's your Variable Gross Margin?	
What's the minimum price you can afford to sell at, to get a trial?	
Does the customer carry competitive products?	
Why should they buy your product?	
What is your Unique Selling Point?	
Which competitive product will your product replace?	
What is the greatest challenge your customer is facing?	
How can you help them meet this challenge?	
What are the idiosyncrasies of the buyer, if any?	
How will you handle that?	

Did you get the sale?   **Yes**   **No**

Lessons Learned:

"We each sell a little piece of happiness. You are elevating someone's spirit in some way, and to do that you have to understand the source of their angst and then you have to frame your product as a solution." - Sonia Marciano

Additional Notes

Chapter 14

KEY MARKETING INSIGHTS

Key Insights

- Understanding the customer

- Marketing and innovation are the key

- Creating a customer

- Making selling superfluous

- Only three ways to grow a business

- The 80/20 Rule

- Life-Time Value of customer

- The price of bad service

- The power of referrals

- Pricing connotes quality

At its heart, Marketing is about the customer: understanding him, connecting with him and meeting his needs and wants. These 10 insights will help you do this well.

1. *"The aim of marketing is to know and understand the customer so well the product or service fits him and sells itself." - Peter Drucker*

People do not know what they want and why they want it. Give them a blank canvas to fill out and they are at a loss for words. Marketing is the tool to help customers realize unrecognized needs.

2. *"Because it is its purpose to create a customer, any business enterprise has two – and only these two – basic functions: marketing and innovation…. Everything else is a cost center… You get paid to create a customer, which is marketing…. And you get paid for creating a new dimension of performance, which is innovation." - Peter Drucker*

The only reason for a company to exist is because it serves someone. Without serving a customer there is no business. Furthermore, the customer is the only one who actually gives you money. Everybody and everything else is an expense. (Entrepreneur and friend, James Steinback, adds: *"The only reason to start a company is that you know you'll regret it for the rest of your life if you don't."*)

3. *So how is this customer created?*

"By understanding what a customer buys is not just a product or service…It is what the product does for the person." - Peter Drucker

"People don't want to buy a quarter-inch drill. They want a quarter-inch hole." - Professor Theodore Levitt

If you are flying from Chicago to LA, what is your need? Your need is to get to LA. Do you really care whether you are flying a Boeing or an Airbus? Do you care what the color the plane is or what the staff is wearing? No. You want to get to LA expeditiously, comfortably and at a reasonable price. People want to buy the result not the process.

4. *"The aim of marketing is to make selling superfluous." - Peter Drucker*

Marketing is the key to connecting with the customer. Selling is just the final link in the process. Let's imagine that you want to buy a laptop and you go to Best Buy. The salesperson shows you a variety of products with different configurations, but nothing seems to stand out for you. In this case, the computer manufacturers have done a poor marketing job. Now compare this to walking into an Apple store. How much selling is involved? Virtually none. That is because Marketing has done what it is supposed to do - make selling superfluous.

5. *There are only three ways to increase a business:*

1) Increase the number of clients

2) Increase the transaction dollars

3) Increase the purchase frequency

This is one of the most insightful observations by marketing whiz and author Jay Abraham. Most companies focus on getting new customers while ignoring those they already have. I cannot think of a worse strategy. This leads to low customer loyalty, a higher churn rate and a significant waste of the marketing dollars. If you want to create a great company, you must first respect and focus on the customers you already have. Find ways to make them come visit you more often and when they visit, find ways to sell them more. Starbucks does a brilliant job of this. Not only does their Customer Loyalty plan gamify the purchasing process, but it also facilitates sales. Customers get excited by the chance to buy more drinks to gain more "stars." Patagonia is another standout. The company provides free refurbishment, replacement and recycling of their own products to any customer who asks, thereby satisfying their own brand values and delighting the customer simultaneously.

6. *20% of your customers will generally produce 80% of your profits.*

This is called the Pareto Principle. Most companies try to do too much, for too many people, and end up doing poorly for just about everybody. I ask my clients to make a list of all their customers and rank them by profitability. Invariably, this analysis shows a small number of customers producing a large percentage of the profits. *Success should not be measured by how many clients you have, but by how well you serve your key customers.*

Even well established companies fall prey to such proliferation and diffusion. P&G, a preeminent marketing company, has bought and developed many brands over the years. They announced recently that they would focus on approximately 80 consumer brands that generate around 90% of the company's sales and 95% of the profits. In order to do this, they will sell off around 100 brands.

The 80/20 principle can also be employed in your approach to your employees. Here is how John Maxwell puts it:

"Love everyone, but give yourself to the 20% in your organization. Encourage the many, mentor the few."

7. *Think Life-Time Value of Customer.*

Another way to develop a better understanding of your key customers is to calculate the LTV (Life-Time Value) of the customer by using the following formula:

*Purchase $ * Frequency Per Year * Number of years*

By analyzing your highest value customers, also called heavy users, you can determine why they buy more, why they buy more often, and why they stay with you longer. This is very valuable data. You can then develop strategies to convert medium users to heavy users, etc. As customers move up the value chain, they are more satisfied and the company is more profitable. Most importantly, focus on your heavy users: keep them in the fold and find ways to sell them more.

8. *Being polite helps, but bad customer service will kill you. Fix the problem the first time.*

Companies spend large amounts of money to attract customers but then do a poor job when customers actually contact them. The following headline, in a recent cartoon,[22] captured this perfectly:

"Your call is very important to us, but not quite important enough to put a human being on the line."

An article[23] titled "Stop Trying To Delight Your Customers" provided the following statistics:

- 25% of the people say that they have had a good customer experience. 23% of them told a friend about this good experience.
- 75% of the people said that they had a bad customer experience. 48% of these told their friends.
- The ratio of people hearing the horror story is 6 times greater than the people hearing the good story.

Therefore, it is a good idea to ensure a good customer experience. A few of the key reasons for customer dissatisfaction were:

- Having to re-explain the problem several times.
- Being transferred from person to person.
- Being asked to switch the medium ("please go to our website").
- Having to call the company several times.

---

[22] Ziggy 2015, Yahoo cartoons
[23] July 2010 Harvard Business Review

None of this will come as a surprise. The key takeaway is to stop talking about how you are going to delight your customers and fix the problem the first time. The strategy may be as simple as empowering your people to make the customers happy and satisfied. Really. Try it.

9. *Referrals are the best way to increase your business.*

A referral from someone you trust lends credibility. As mentioned in a previous chapter, the Net Promoter Score is used by many companies to measure exactly how likely a customer is to recommend a product or firm. Social media has made referrals easy and compelling as witnessed by the advent of services like Yelp. Studies have shown that clients from referrals stay longer and are less concerned about price. *Going viral is the equivalent of achieving referral nirvana.*

10. *Price connotes quality.*

Entrepreneurs, especially when they are first starting, focus on getting customers by cutting prices. You need to remember that price connotes quality. Cutting prices can hurt your brand. Would a Lacoste T-shirt have the same appeal if you could find it at Walmart on sale? This strategy was actually tried some years ago and it almost ruined the brand. The company went back to its origins, limited distribution, focused on quality and increased prices. They have done very well since.

Years ago I happened to be in charge of Ghirardelli chocolate. At that time Ghirardelli did not make much money because it had low prices to garner higher sales. Market research indicated that Ghirardelli had taste ratings similar to that of Godiva chocolate. The team redesigned the package, gave it the feel, quality and image of a luxury brand and increased prices. The business has done well over the years.

Assignment: What ideas and thoughts did these insights provoke?

Chapter 15

MARKETING PLAN
V1

"Failing to plan is planning to fail." - Alan Lakein

"To accomplish great things, we must not only act, but also dream; not only plan, but also believe." - Anatole France

"Plans rarely stay the same, and are scrapped or adjusted as needed. Be stubborn about the vision, but flexible with your plan."
  - John C. Maxwell

~~~~~~~~

Key Topics in this Chapter

- Key components of the Marketing Plan

- Supporting data checklist

- Use of analogs, antilogs, assumptions, research

- Where to next?

You've stayed up all night, worked late, talked to friends, read countless reviews and thought about your business from every angle. You have a clearer sense of the customers, the industry, its segments and your competitors. You have developed a positioning, branding and pricing strategy for your business and identified the channels of distribution. You know how you will sell. Congratulations on a job well done.

Key Components of the Marketing Plan

From Chapter 2, you will recall that the final business plan will be 10 pages, while the pitch will be 10 slides. They will both have the same focus.

1. **Problem / Solution**
2. **Product**
3. **Customer**
4. **Competition**
5. **Marketing & Sales**

 **Marketing Plans**

6. **Business Model**
7. **Financial Plan**
8. **Funding**
9. **Team**
10. **Timeline**

The first five slides / questions comprise your Marketing Plan. You have collected an enormous amount of data on these subjects. Your challenge now is to distill this knowledge in a clear, cogent and compelling manner in five pages.

This will be Version 1 of your marketing plan. You will keep updating and revising this plan until you launch.

Supporting Data Checklist

These checklists are designed to help you marshal your thoughts.

1. *Problem / Solution (Chapter 2):* What is the problem? What is your solution? Be sure to make the problem come alive. Your solution must solve the problem and provide value to the customer.

2. *Product (Chapter 2):* Describe your product vividly and why this is <u>the</u> product to solve the problem. *You will grab, or lose, the audience with your answers to these two questions.*

3. *Customer / Consumer (Chapters 7, 8, 10)*

Key Demographics   Key Psychographics

° Age   ° Environmental Focus
° Gender   ° Lifestyle (Active, Sedentary etc.)

- ° Occupation
- ° Income
- ° Education
- ° Ethnicity
- ° Marital Status
- ° Children
- ° College Education
- ° Geographic Location

- ° Social Focus (high, medium, low)
- ° Tech Savvy (high, medium, low)
- ° Image Conscious
- ° Financial Focus
- ° Key beliefs
- ° What is most important to them?
- ° What do they fear most?
- ° What do they read?
- ° Where do they travel?
- ° What shows do they like?

Marketing Utility
- o Functional =   %, Social =   %, Emotional =   %, Total = 100%.
- o Explain in one sentence what you believe your customer is seeking from your product.

Beachhead Target
- o Describe your beachhead target in detail.

Customer Persona
- o Make your customer come to life by writing a few words describing him.
- o Draw a sketch of this person.

4. *Competition (Chapter 9)*
- o Industry Size and Growth
- o Market Segments
- o Key Competitors: Share of market, trends, strengths and weaknesses for each competitor
- o Market segment map (The map for Gap is an excellent model)
- o Opportunities

5. *Marketing and Sales (Chapters 11, 12, 13)*

   Positioning Statement
   - ▪ Who is your target customer?
   - ▪ What is your product?
   - ▪ Why should your target customer buy your "competitive advantage" i.e. your "point of difference?"
   - ▪ What is your positioning statement?

   Brand
   - ▪ Which of these attributes does your brand have (as explained in Chapter 12)?
     - • Short
     - • Distinct
     - • Sounds good
     - • Suggests compelling benefit
     - • Breaks the rules
     - • Easy to say
     - • Is acceptable worldwide
   - ▪ Why did you choose it?
   - ▪ What is your tagline?

- Is it memorable?
- Does it capture the essence of your brand?

Pricing
- What is your pricing and why?
- How does it compare with the competitors?
- Does it accurately reflect the value that you are providing?

Promotional Plan
- What media will you be using and why?
- What is your budget?
- If your plan is to rely on social media, be sure to develop a detailed plan and why you think it will be effective.

Distribution channels
- What will you be using and why?

Selling strategy
- What is your selling pitch?
- Why is it good for the customer?
- Why should they buy your product?
- Why should they do business with you?

6. *New Assignment:* Develop a rough sales and income forecast for 3 and 12 months.
    o You know your pricing and distribution channels. Develop a rough sales forecast.
    o Rationale for this forecast?
    o For income, use the best estimates you can come up with.
       - Even though rough, these numbers provide a sanity check at this point.
       - By the time your final plan is complete you will have fine-tuned these numbers even more, thereby providing a higher degree of confidence.

Use of Analogs, Antilogs,
Assumptions, Research

Throughout your work, be on the lookout for analogs and antilogs. You will recall that an analog is a business idea that you want to emulate and an antilog is one that you want to avoid. Make sure you have a dashboard of all your assumptions that need to be verified.

Let's take stock of what has been done to date and what still needs to be done by answering these questions.

- What are the analogs that you have embraced for your product?
- Why did you choose these analogs?
- What are the antilogs that you have chosen?
- Why did you choose these antilogs?
- What assumptions, Leaps of Faith, are embedded in your work?
- What is your research plan to validate these assumptions?
- What is the timetable for this research?

ASSIGNMENT: Write out your marketing plan. The more detail the better.

Problem/ Solution:

Product/ Service:

Customer:

Competition:

Marketing & Sales:

Analogs:

Antilogs:

Research Needed To Be Done:

Where to Now?

You have indeed done a lot of work and should be proud of your achievements. Take a deep breath and pat yourself on the back. You have learned many new things, about business, your teammates and, I suspect, about yourself.

At this stage you have a good understanding of the problem you are solving, the product you will develop, the competitive set and your marketing plan. This is the foundation for any business. "No Customer, No Business" is our mantra that bears repeating.

Where do you go next? You will now turn your attention to the operating side of the business, its structure, costs and profitability. Remember a business cannot survive long without being profitable. You will need to look at each assumption critically. Every step of the way you must ask: Is this the best way to do this? What else is possible? How can I make the business better?

"You must stick to your conviction, but be ready to abandon your assumptions" - Denis Watley

Take a day off and then plow straight ahead.

PART III

OPERATIONS

In this section, you will learn the financial concepts fundamental to understanding the health of a business. Even though some numbers and simple arithmetic are involved, I have tried to make everything easy to understand. You will review each element of your business, including costs, and analyze ways to improve them. You will then determine how much money you will need to start your business and complete the operations section of the business plan. By the end, you will have nearly all the pieces that you will need to get started.

Chapter 16

BASIC FINANCIAL CONCEPTS

"Rule No. 1: Never lose money. Rule No. 2: Never forget Rule No. 1." - Warren Buffett

"Don't live like a CEO when you're still a sandwich artist."
- Sophia Amoruso, #GIRLBOSS

"Many small businesses would rather face an angry barbarian horde than tackle their cash flow statement or price a new product." - Nicole Fende, How to be a Finance Rock Star

~~~~~~~~

Key Topics in this Chapter

- Revisit Chapter 6: Business Model

- The Three Key Financial Statements

    o The Profit & Loss Statement

    o The Balance Sheet

    o The Cash Flow Statement

- Key Financial Ratios

- Trends Tell The Tale

- Competitive Comparison

- How does this apply to me?

- Assignment: Develop your financial statements

A few of you may be math wizards while some may have a touch of Arithmophobia, which is a fear of numbers. For the wizards, this chapter will be a good refresher. The rest of you should also relax. If you do the calculations alongside me, you'll be pleasantly surprised by how quickly you learn. Focus on learning the concepts. Don't sweat the small stuff.

Financial statements and ratios are the scorecard of a business. They help you understand the business, tell you when things are going well and flash warning signs when needed.

Marketing with its focus on brands, visualization and connecting with customers has a touch of poetry. Finance is grittier, more real, and while it may not quite nourish the soul, it is necessary to meet the temporal necessities.

Revisit Chapter 6: Business Model

This is a good time to revisit the "Business Model" discussion in Chapter 6. Let us recap the key learning: The financial purpose of a business is to make money. You sell a product or service for a certain price, which creates *Revenues*. You incur *Costs* to generate these revenues. The difference between the two is *Profits*. This is the fundamental equation.

$$\boxed{\textbf{Revenues} - \textbf{Costs} = \textbf{Profits}}$$

The Three Key Financial Statements

There are three key financial statements – *P&L, Balance Sheet* and *Cash Flow* - that fall under the discipline of Accounting. They will help you answer questions such as: How much revenue did the business generate? What did it cost? What does the business own and owe? Does it make money?

We will use Costco's financial statements to delve into these questions because many of you are likely to be familiar with the company and its business model. However, this analysis can be applied to any business.

Please note that all the financial data in this chapter has been obtained from Yahoo Finance (finance.yahoo.com).

The P&L (Profit and Loss Statement)

The P&L, also called the income statement, tells us whether a business made money or not during a certain period. It is generally calculated monthly and most public companies report their results every quarter.

The most recent *annual* results for Costco are:

Income Statement (P&L) for Period Ended Aug. 31, 2014*

	Millions of $
Total Revenue	112,640
Cost of Revenue	98,458
Gross Profit (Revenue - Cost)	**14,182**
Operating Expenses	
Selling, General & Administrative	10,899
Other Expenses	63
Total Operating Expenses	**10,962**
Operating Income	3,220
Other Income	90
Earnings before Income & Taxes (EBIT)	**3,310**
Interest Expense	113
Earnings before Taxes (EBT)	**3,197**
Income Tax	1,109
Net Income	**2,058**

The fiscal year for most companies coincides with the calendar year. Some companies, especially in retailing, will match their fiscal year to their business cycle. Costco's fiscal year ended on August 31, 2014. What does this statement tell us?

- Sales (Revenues) for these 12 months were $112.6 billion.
- The cost of selling the products (Cost of Goods) was $98.5 billion.
- This resulted in a Gross Profit of $14.2 billion.
- Their main overhead expense for Selling, General and Administrative (SG&A) amounted to $10.9 billion.
- After deducting this expense, the company had an Operating Income of $3.2 billion.
- They had an Interest expense of $113 million and paid $1.1 billion of taxes.
- The Net Income, also called the bottom line, was $2.1 billion

*All financial numbers are from Yahoo Finance

** Numbers may not add up due to rounding and minor omissions.

Think of the P&L as a *movie* called "A Year in the Life of Costco." It tells us, in gripping detail, how much was sold, what it cost, what was paid to the banks and what the tax collector bit off. At the end of the saga, we discover that Costco survived and actually made $2.1 billion of profits. Stay tuned for the sequel next year.

The Balance Sheet

The Balance Sheet is not a movie but a *snapshot* of another part of the operations. It captures what a company *owns* ("Assets") and *owes* ("Liabilities") on the day of the photograph. Let's look at Costco again.

Balance Sheet for Period Ended August 31, 2014

ASSETS	Millions of $	LIABILITIES	Millions of $
Current Assets		**Current Liabilities**	
Cash & Investments	7,315	Accounts Payable	11,937
Net Receivables	1,817	Other Current Liabilities	2,475
Inventory	8,456		
Total Current Assets	**17,588**	**Total Current Liabilities**	**14,412**
Fixed Assets		**Long Term Liabilities**	
Property, Plant, & Equipment	14,830	Long Term Debt	5,093
Other Assets	606	Other	1,216
		Stockholder's Equity	**12,303**
Total Fixed Assets	**15,436**	**Total Long Term Liabilities**	**18,612**
TOTAL ASSETS	**33,024**	**TOTAL LIABILITIES**	**33,024**

The first thing to note about the Balance Sheet is its wonderful symmetry:

Assets = Liabilities

This is *always* the case. *What a company owns always equals what it owes.* Let's peruse further.

There are generally two broad kinds of *Assets*:

1. *Current Assets* are considered to be more liquid and will convert into cash in less than 12 months. Costco had $17.6 billion of current assets divided as follows:
    a. $7.3 billion of Cash and Short Term Investments. This money can be used quickly if needed.
    b. Receivables totaled $1.8 billion. Most sales at Costco are paid for by a credit card. They will collect the cash in a few days from the banks and credit card company. In the meanwhile, this balance is labeled a receivable - money that they anticipate receiving.
    c. Inventories are all those items piled up in the Costco stores and warehouses, waiting to be sold to you. These totaled $8.5 billion.

Fixed Assets are longer term in nature. Costco's main fixed assets are its stores and land, amounting to a total of $15.4 billion.

By adding these two kinds of assets, we see that Costco had $33.0 billion of *Total Assets*.

Looking at the Liabilities, we note that they too totaled $33.0 billion. Let's examine the components.

1. *Current Liabilities,* totaling $14.4 billion, are moneys that Costco must pay out within 12 months. Of this, the Accounts Payable of $11.9 billion is what they owe to suppliers.

2. *Long Term Liabilities* are payments that are due beyond 12 months and include the Long Term Debt of about $5.1 billion. This is a rather small amount given the size of Costco and reflects its conservative approach to business.

3. The third account called *Shareholders' Equity* equals $12.3 billion. Many people often struggle with this category. Let's demystify this.

    a. *What exactly is Shareholders' Equity?* People put in money to start a company for which they receive shares which reflects their proportional ownership. Over time the company generates an income. Some of this is paid to the shareholders in the form of dividends. The remainder - called Retained Earnings - is kept in the business to grow the business. Shareholders' Equity, therefore, is the sum total of the money that the shareholders have put into the company. It includes the original investment as well as the profits that have been reinvested in the business.

    b. *Why is Shareholders' Equity a liability and not an asset owned by the shareholders?* A business is a separate legal entity from its shareholders. From Costco's point of view, the shareholders' equity is a liability because that money does not belong to the company; rather it is owed to its shareholders. From the shareholders' point of view, this money is indeed an asset, and therefore, will be reflected on their *personal* balance sheets.

    c. *Costco's Shareholders' Equity is $33 billion but its market value is more than $60 billion; what is the right number?* They both are. Here is a good analogy: A person bought a house for $200,000 several years ago and it now has a market value of $400,000. The $200,000 represents his cost; this is similar to Shareholders' Equity. The $400,000 represents today's market value and this is akin to the market value of Costco's stock.

The Cash Flow Statement

The P&L and Balance Sheet are easy to understand and most businessmen focus on these statements. However, the most important financial statement is the *Cash Flow* statement, because it deals with Cash, which is the oxygen of the business.

The concept of cash flow is easy. It is like your checkbook. For each action ask yourself: *Will this use up or generate cash? Will my checkbook balance increase or decrease?*

What are some things that *use* up cash?
- Salaries
- Rent, utilities, taxes
- Inventory - since you have to buy goods in order to resell them
- Buying assets such as equipment or land
- Paying dividends

What activities *generate* cash?
- Sales
- A loan from a bank. (Yes, you will have to pay it back, but the act of getting the loan brings in cash.)
- Reducing Inventory - this way less cash is tied up.
- Reducing Receivables - this is the same as collecting on a loan that you have made.
- Increasing Payables - you pay more slowly and hang on to cash longer.
- Depreciation - this is a bit complex but here is a simple explanation. When a business buys equipment, it has to pay for it immediately. This expense occurs under "buying assets" and is an immediate use of cash. The cost of buying this equipment cannot be deducted as an expense right away. Tax rules dictate the number of years an asset must be depreciated over. When a company subsequently depreciates this asset, it

becomes an expense and therefore reduces taxes. This reduction in taxes becomes a positive cash flow. Convoluted? Sue the IRS. It is their tax code after all.

The Cash Flow Statement looks at both the P&L and the change that has occurred in the Balance Sheet from the last period.

Here is Costco's cash flow statement for last year.

CASH FLOW ACTIVITY (Year ending 8/31/14)	$ (Million)	CASH FLOW Generate "+", Use "-"
Operating Activities		
Net Income - made money in 2014.	2,058	+
Depreciation - as previously explained.	1,029	+
Receivables were unchanged. Hence no impact.	0	
Payables were higher. Used other people's money.	529	+
Inventories were higher, used more cash.	-563	-
All Other	901	+
Cash Flow from Operating Activities	**3,984**	++
Investing Activities - mainly for capital expenditure.	**-2,093**	--
Financing Activities		
Paid Dividends	-584	-
Bought back stock	-296	-
All other	-1	-
Total Financing Activities	**-797**	--
Total Cash Flow in 2014	**1,094**	++

A quick summary: Costco made $2.1 billion in income and had a total operating cash flow of about $4.0 billion. It used $2.1 billion to finance its growth and another $0.8 billion to pay dividends and buy back its own stock. All said, it increased its cash position by $1.1 billion in 2014.

Key Financial Ratios

Key financial ratios are a quick and handy way to understand the health of a business. We will do three things with these ratios:
1. Learn how to calculate these ratios.
2. Look at the trends and see what they tell us.
3. Compare the ratios across competitors to better understand the industry, the company and emerging trends.

This is similar to how you monitor your health: you measure your pulse and blood pressure periodically, keep key records and then compare your data against relevant benchmarks. Let's continue our analysis of Costco.

- *Gross Margin Ratio:* Formula = Gross Margin / Revenues
    - The Gross Margin is obtained by subtracting Cost of Goods from Revenues.
    - Cost of Goods is the direct cost of what you are selling, without adding any marketing, overhead, or financing costs.
    - In 2014, the Gross Margin Ratio for Costco was: 14.2/ 112.6 = about 13%.
    - A 13% Gross Margin means that Costco generates $13 of gross profit for every $100 in sales.
    - Different industries often have different gross margins. Branded food businesses like Frosted Flakes can have margins approaching 80%, while software companies may exceed 90%.

- *Net Income (NI) Margin: Formula = Net Income / Sales*
    - Costco's NI Margin = 2.1/112.6 or about 2%.
    - For every $100 of sales, Costco makes a bottom line profit of about $2. Costco's business model is to price low, sell a lot, keep overheads low and grow.

- *Return on Assets (ROA): Formula = Net Income / Total Assets*
    - This measure indicates the amount of profit generated for each dollar invested in the business.
    - Costco's ROA = 2.1/ 33 or about 6%.

- *Return on Equity (ROE): Formula = Net Income / Shareholders' Equity*
    - This ratio calculates the return the shareholders are making on their investment.
    - Costco ROE = 2.1/12.3 or about 17%.

- *# of Days of Receivables: Formula = Total Receivables / Daily Sales*
    - You want to keep receivables as low as possible.
    - A good way to track this performance is to calculate how many days of receivables are outstanding.
    - For Costco this is = 1,817 / (112,640/365) = a little less than 6 days.
    - This number is so low because sales are paid for with cash, checks, or credit cards. They convert the checks and credit card sales into cash very quickly.

- *Inventory Turnover: Formula = Cost of Goods / Inventory*
    - Inventory also uses up cash so you want to turn over (sell) the inventory as rapidly as possible.
    - For Costco this is = 98,458 / 8456 = or about 12 times a year

There are many other ratios, but these are the key ratios that you should focus on to get started.

Trends Tell the Tale

The next part of the analysis is to see how these ratios are changing over time. This is like taking an annual physical, which tells us what is going well and what needs attention.

Costco: Millions of $, unless otherwise noted

From P&L	2014	2013	2012
Revenue	112,640	105,156	99,137
Revenue Growth from Yr. Ago	7%	6%	
Cost of Goods	98,458	91,948	86,823
Gross Profit	14,182	13,208	12,314
Net Income	2,058	2,039	1,709
Net Income Growth from Yr. Ago	1%	19%	

From Balance Sheet	2014	2013	2012
Cash & Short Term Investments	7,315	6,124	4,854
Receivables	1,817	1,822	1,576
Inventory	8,456	7,894	7,096
Total Assets	33,024	30,283	27,140
Shareholders' Equity	12,303	10,833	12,361

Key Financial Ratios (all calculated from above numbers)

	2014	2013	2012
Gross Margin Ratio (%)	12.6%	12.6%	12.4%
Net Income Ratio (%)	1.8%	1.9%	1.7%
Return on Assets - ROA - (%)	6.2%	6.7%	6.3%
Return on Equity - ROE - (%)	16.7%	18.8%	13.8%
Day's Receivables (days)	5.9	6.3	5.8
Inventory Turnover (times/yr.)	11.6X	11.6X	12.2X

Here is what these trends tell me:
- Sales continue to grow at about 6-7% per year.
- Net Income growth slowed down to only 1% last year. Why? Look into it.
- The cash position is healthy with more than $7 billion readily available.
- The Gross Margin remains around 12.5% which is in keeping with Costco's pricing policy.
- The Net Income margin also remains stable at around 2% while the ROA hovers in the 6-7% range. Looks stable.
- ROE jumped significantly in 2013, but has leveled off in 2014; check.
- They continue to do an excellent job keeping receivables low and turning their inventory almost every month.
- Looks like the patient, oops, the company is holding steady but we need to check out a few things.

Competitive Comparison

The final plank in understanding a business well is to do compare it with competitors. To understand Costco better, let us now also examine Walmart and Target.

Latest Fiscal Year, Millions of $, unless otherwise stated

From P&L	Costco	Walmart	Target
Revenue	112,640	485,561	72,618
Cost of Goods	98,458	365,086	51,278
Gross Profit / Margin	14,182	120,565	21,340
Net Income	2,058	16,363	2,449

From Balance Sheet	Costco	Walmart	Target
Cash & Short Term Investments	7,315	9,135	2,210
Receivables	1,817	6,778	-
Inventory	8,456	45,141	8,790
Total Assets	33,024	203,706	41,404
Shareholders' Equity	12,303	81,394	13,997
Market Value (Billions $)	64	252	52

Key Financial Ratios (calculated)	Costco	Walmart	Target
Gross Margin Ratio (%)	12.6%	24.8%	29.3%
Net Income Ratio (%)	1.8%	3.4%	3.4%
Return on Equity - ROE - (%)	16.7%	20.1%	17.5%
Return on Assets - ROA - (%)	6.2%	8.0%	5.9%
Day's Receivables (days)	5.9	5.1	0
Inventory Turnover (times/yr.)	11.6X	8.1X	5.8X

Please note: Costco is as of 8/31/14; Walmart and Target as of 1/31/15

This is what I learned from this analysis:

- Walmart is about five times the size of Costco and Target.
- Walmart and Target both have higher Gross Margin and Net Income ratios than Costco because they have different business models.
- Walmart has the strongest ROE and ROA.
- Given that Sam's is a poor second to Costco and is included in Walmart's results, the base Walmart business is even stronger than these numbers indicate.
- Target seems to have managed to eliminate its net receivables, which is remarkable. How did they do this? Worth checking into.

- Costco does the best job of turning over its inventory, keeping only about a month's worth on hand. Target seems to have twice as much inventory; there may be room for improvement there.

With a bit of practice, you can learn a significant amount about any business with these simple analyses.

How does this apply to me?

That's a reasonable question. As an entrepreneur you have to know a little bit about a lot of things. By learning the basic concepts outlined here you will develop a good grasp of fundamental finance and financial statements. More importantly, you will develop a sense of what is important and what you should be paying attention to. Below are a few things that you should remember:

- Cash is the oxygen that will allow you to survive. Pay close attention to it.
- Sales are great to have but only if you can collect the receivables.
- Keep receivables and inventory as low as possible.
- Extend payables as much as possible.
- Gross Margins can range from 10% to 90% depending on your industry and business model. Why not aim for a higher Gross Margin?
- Keep close track of all expenses. At the start, especially, you cannot afford much overhead. Travel light.
- Every business has a few ratios that are the key to performance. Figure out what these are for your business and monitor them assiduously.

Assignment: Develop your Financial Statements

Spend more time thinking of Year 1. Years 2 and 3 can be rough estimates.

P&L – 3 Years

Profit and Loss Statement	Year 1	Year 2	Year 3
Total Revenues / Sales			
Cost of Goods Sold			
Variable Gross Profit (Revenue – C/G)			
Other Expenses			
Selling, General & Admin (SG&A)			
Other Business Expenses			
Interest Expenses			
Taxes			
Total Other Expenses			
Net Income **(Variable Gross Profit – Other Expenses)**			

Balance Sheet – Year End	Year 1	Year 2	Year 3
ASSETS			
Cash and Investments			
Receivables			
Inventory			
Total Current Assets			
Property, Plant , & Equipment			
Other long term assets			
Total Fixed Assets			
TOTAL ASSESTS (Current + Fixed)			
LIABILTIES			
Accounts Payable			
Other Current (less than 12 months) Liabilities			
Total Current Liabilities			
Long Term Debt			
Shareholder's Equity			
Total Long Tem Liabilities			
TOTAL LIABILITES (Current + Long term)			

While you are not a CPA as yet, you have learned the basics of accounting quite well. Now let's get on with refining your business model.

Additional Notes

Chapter 17

REFINING YOUR BUSINESS MODEL

"A disruptive innovation is a technologically simple innovation in the form of a product, service, or business model that takes root in a tier of the market that is unattractive to the established leaders in an industry." - Clayton Christensen

"By simply capitalizing on core strengths and knowledge, companies and entrepreneurs can engage in an emerging business model that will enable them to create - and demonstrate - real, sustainable social impact in society." - Muhammad Yunus

"The best way to refine an interpretation is by getting out and performing." - Joshua Bell

~~~~~~~~

Key Topics in this Chapter

- Business Models Come in All Flavors

- Revenues

- Cost of Goods

- Overhead Structures

- Plan B

- Assignment: Refine your Business Model

By now, you have a clear idea of your product, its price, how you will market it and the overhead structure you will need to execute your plan. You have also developed rough financials that most likely indicate the business growing with time and achieving profitability. In essence, you have developed your business model.

You will now examine the key components of this model in order to understand it better and enhance it. We will present several examples that we hope will spark thought as you refine your model.

"My sweet spot is figuring out how to make a product that people love and how to refine it to make them love it more. All the rest is business noise." - Nolan Bushnell

Business Models Come In All Flavors

A good business model answers the question: How will you make money? It does this by first examining the revenues and expenses of a business. This is what we will focus on in this chapter. You also have to determine how much capital you will need and when the business will break even. This we will tackle in the next chapter.

Let's start with two fundamental variables of the business model: 1) The bundle of value and 2) Price.

At one end, there is The Four Seasons Hotel delivering a high bundle of value, in the form of a high quality product supported with excellent service, charging more than $500 a night. At the other end, there is Motel 6 delivering a more modest bundle of value, but still offering a small clean room, limited service, for only $50 a night. Both of these are successful business models.

In between these two ends there are an almost infinite number of price and value points possible. Marriott, alone, offers 19 hotel brands ranging from The Ritz Carlton and the Bvlgari brand on the high end to the Residence Inn and Springhill Suites on the more affordable end.

Financial ratios can also help us discern differing business models.

Margins (% of Sales)

	Gross Margin	Operating Overhead	Operating Income
Whole Foods	35%	28%	7%
Supervalu	15%	12%	3%
Macy's	40%	30%	10%
TJ Maxx	28%	16%	12%

* Latest Fiscal Years for the companies as of April 15, 2015 from Yahoo Finance

Whole Foods and Supervalu are similar size businesses. Whole Foods offers higher quality products with more attentive service but at higher prices. Therefore, it has higher gross margin and overhead expense ratios. Supervalu owns several brands including Cub and Fresh Farm with a focus on the value segment. Its prices are lower and its service is modest, which is then reflected in lower gross margins and overheads.

Macy's and TJ Maxx are both clothing and home goods retailers. Macy's is a full service retailer, charging higher prices and providing high in-store support. As a result, Macy's has higher gross margin and operating expenses. TJ Maxx on the other hand, is known for its low prices and limited in-store service, which result in lower gross margins and overhead expenses.

In our examples, all the companies are profitable despite different pricing strategies. Businesses with both low and high prices can be profitable or unprofitable. The profitability depends on the robustness of the overall business model, not on whether you choose a low or high pricing strategy.

Revenues

The two elements of gross margin are revenues and cost of goods. Revenues in turn have two components - price and unit volume.

Price

It is human tendency to drop the price initially because you are desperate to generate sales. This is not an unreasonable instinct, but it may not necessarily be good for the brand. I found this out with one of the first businesses I was in charge of, Ghirardelli chocolates. Raising prices consistent with the quality and image of the brand increased sales. Warren Buffett is known to give his operating companies wide latitude in running their businesses. Sometimes, though, he retains the right to make the pricing decision, because he believes that he has greater objectivity than the company's management. Years ago when he bought See's Candy he did exactly that and raised prices annually. Needless to say, the company and Mr. Buffett have both done well. Bottom line, do not be afraid to price appropriately.

As you think about pricing, remember that the price of a product is situation specific. Bottled water costs $0.25 at Costco, $2 in a vending machine and $5 in a fancy restaurant. Uber has been creative with its surge-pricing model. It is a fancy way of capitalizing on the basic law of economics: *the greater the demand, the higher the price.*

Volume

It is imperative that you get trial for your product up front. That is what coupons are meant to do. Groupon can, under the right circumstances, be a good trial device. The temporarily lowered price can induce potential customers to give the product a try.

The Freemium model appears to work well with web based businesses. Dropbox, Google Drive, Microsoft One Drive, LinkedIn, Spotify, Evernote, SurveyMonkey and MailChimp have used this model effectively.

You must develop the right trial devices to get potential customers to try your product and by satisfying them, you can develop permanent customers and build volume.

Cost of Goods

The best way to scrutinize costs is to look at every line item and ask yourself: is there a better or less expensive way to do this? While the cost of goods relates to the raw material, this approach should be applied to every element of your business.

Let's use Starbucks as an example to do this analysis. Have you ever wondered what the actual cost of the latte in your hand really is? Let's go find the answer.

A quick review of the reported Starbucks financial statements shows sales of $17 billion, a gross margin of 58% and an operating income margin of 19%. We can deduce that this is a highly profitable business model that focuses on high prices and high service. In trying to dig deeper, I came across a blog called Consumeronomics[24], which had this wonderful graphic from *The Wall Street Journal.*

---

[24] http://consumeronomics.anoj.net/2013/09/caffeinonomics-1-pricing-cup-of.html

Pricing Grounds | Starbucks grande latte in China

Total: $4.80

Other operating expenses	$0.23	5%
Equipment costs	0.17	4%
Tax	0.24	5%
General and administration	0.28	6%
Labor	0.41	9%
Raw materials	0.64	13%
Store operating expenses	0.72	15%
Profit	0.85	18%
Rent	1.25	26%

Note: Figures don't add up to 100% due to rounding.

Source: SmithStreet   The Wall Street Journal

Costs do vary by country, but this snapshot gives us a good idea of the economics of a Starbucks' latte. It shows a profit of 18%, which ties into the reported earnings of the company. The raw material, which is the coffee, milk, cup, lid and holder, costs only $0.64, or about 13% of sales.

Rent comes in at 26%, which reflects their premium locations and décor. Labor, store operating expenses and equipment add up to another 28%, which are needed to deliver a high quality experience.

Study this chart. Then develop the same level of detail for your business and examine every line of expense. That is how you refine your model.

Overhead Structures

Once you have thoroughly examined your revenue and cost of goods structure, turn your focus to overhead costs with a critical eye. Especially at the outset, defer any non-essential expenditure. Keep costs variable as long as possible. Rent or lease, don't buy for now. Keep your gunpowder - aka cash - dry as long as possible.

Let us study three examples of overhead structures, low, high and virtual, to spark further thought. Even though we are using some large companies as examples, this thought process is applicable to any business.

Low Overhead Structure: Southwest Airlines

Southwest has always competed on price and pioneered the best low cost structure of any airline in America. However, just as importantly, they do a superior job on customer service. They treat their employees well who then like working there.

A little bit of airline history is in order. Prior to the deregulation of airlines in 1978, the government set airfares so everyone had the same pricing. Business travelers were the main customers and airlines competed on service and frequency of departure. It was a cozy gentlemanly atmosphere until deregulations unleashed a brave new world. Virtually every American airline has gone through bankruptcy, sometimes more than once. They have been plagued by bad morale, layoffs and occasional strikes. Competition has led to lower fares but the flying experience has suffered.

Southwest, in contrast, has managed to fly above this turbulence. They have had 41 consecutive years of profitability. Herb Kelleher's leadership had much to do with this, but it is their business model that has really set them apart. Their cost / mile is the lowest in the industry. How do they do it?

- *Simplicity*: They use only one kind of aircraft - the Boeing 737. Most airlines have several versions of Boeing and Airbus aircrafts. Different planes require different training, pilots, handling procedures and spare parts, all of which add up to complexity, headaches and cost.
- *Fast Loading*: They do not assign seats - rather people board by group numbers, which turns out to be the speediest process of all. Fast, efficient and friendly. What a concept!
- *30-minute turnaround*: Most airlines take 60 minutes from the time they land to the time they take off again. Southwest, because they use only one plane, does this in half the time
- *Higher ROA*: The airplane is a very expensive asset. Less time on the ground means more time in the air, which means greater utilization and a higher Return on Assets (ROA).
- *High Morale*: One of my students interned and then worked there. Her stories all pointed to a culture in which people loved doing what they were doing. If you want to learn more, I heartily recommend *Nuts*[25], a book that recounts the story of the airline's growth, philosophy and culture

Southwest is an excellent example of a low price, low overhead and good service model.

High Overhead Structure: Luxury Hotels

"For a few thousand dollars a night, guests are exposed to striking sunsets, very expensive spa treatments and meals prepared by top-rated chefs." - Trip Advisor, 10 Best Hotels in the World.

When you charge that much money, the service better be exceptional which necessitates a high overhead structure. Hilary Stockton in reviewing[26] 5 star hotels enumerated the things that captured her attention: Attentive, discreet and constant service; personalization; complementary house car; in room Nespresso; pool service....

In the United States, The Four Seasons and the Ritz Carlton epitomize luxury. Knowledgeable travelers believe that Asian chains such as The Peninsula and Mandarin provide even better service.

However, for the cognoscenti, The Oberoi Chain of India may be the leading purveyor of luxury and esoteric experiences. Their website shows a couple gazing at the Taj Mahal with the tagline "Welcome to the Oberoi Experiences." The copy continues: "Serene surroundings. Luxurious rooms. And legendary service." And should you care for a massage, be prepared to answer: "Would you prefer an Ayurvedic, Balinese, Hawaiian, or Thai massage?'

The high price, high service, high overhead model, when done right, works exceptionally well.

A Virtual Model

You have no doubt been wondering how does a starting entrepreneur develop a strong operating structure on a tiny budget. The Walden Paddlers case[27] that I have used in class should cheer you up.

Paul was in his 40s when he found himself with an opportunity to start a new company. (Translation: He got laid off with some severance dollars.) He decided to combine his passion for the outdoors with his desire to help preserve the environment. So Paul designed kayaks with recycled plastics. The elegance of this model lay in the alliances that Paul formed with like-minded companies based on *shared values, respect and trust*. This network included producers of recycled plastics, manufacturers who had excess capacity and retailers like REI. They all appreciated Paul's commitment to them, as well as to the kayak buyers. He generated sales exceeding a million dollars with only four people on the payroll.

---

[25] Freiberg, Kevin & Jackie. *Nuts!* New York: Bard Press, 1996.
[26] "What Makes a 5-Star Hotel? Top 10 Things to Look For" by Hilary Stockton
http://travelsort.com/blog/what-makes-a-5-star-hotel-top-10-things-to-look-for
[27] Case UVA-ENT-0027 by Professor Andrea Larson of the Darden School of Business Administration, 1997.

Many people want to be associated with a cause. Can you find like-minded fellow travelers to come along with you on your journey? Why not extend your reach with a virtual circle?

Plan B

It would not surprise me if your business model has gone through a few iterations from when you first started and perhaps even from when you started reading this chapter.

Businesses that survive and become successful often do so because they keep iterating their model until it clicks with the customer. Even with all the work you are doing, and will do by the time you launch, you will need to keep pivoting your business until it takes firm hold. It is worth remembering that so-called overnight successes have tried many things, over a number of years, before getting their business model right.

There are many wonderful reminders of this process in *"Getting to Plan B – Breaking Through To A Better Business Model"* by Mullins and Komisar. We share a few examples below.

Google built this marvelous search engine but by itself it did not make any money. They licensed it to others like Yahoo, but that yielded limited revenues. They thought about letting companies sell ads to their users but this conflicted with their notion of doing no evil. The model then evolved through a series of iterations to the pay per click that we know it to be today. Maybe it was Plan F that finally worked.

eBay started as a hobby with the founder trying to sell some "junk" online. He then decided to develop a place - a market if you will - where sellers and buyers could interact and eBay would facilitate the transaction. He charged a small fee for listing and a larger fee for "success." He had a competitor "OnSale" with an almost similar model with one major difference. OnSale took possession of the goods, which made their cost of goods much higher. While eBay had a gross margin of around 80%, OnSale had only 10%.

A little twist here, a little tweak there and suddenly it all makes sense. What part of the alphabet are you on - B, C, D, or...? Keep going.

Assignment: Refine your Business Model

Yes, some of these questions are sometimes repetitive, but they bear repeating and rethinking. Need a sharp pencil for these calculations.

- **Evaluate: Bundle of Value / Price**

  o Clearly define your bundle of value:

  o Why is it compelling for the customer?

  o What is your price?

  o How does your proposition fit within the competitive set?

  o What is your Unique Selling Proposition?

  o Should you charge a higher price?

- **Volume forecasting**

  o How much volume will you do in Year 1?

  o How will you get trial?

  o How long will the trial program last?

  o How much will it cost?

  o How will you make it effective?

- **Cost of goods?**

  o What is your Cost of Goods?

  o How did you arrive at this?

o Can the costs be reduced by tweaking your model?

o What is your Gross Margin?

o Is it appropriate for your bundle of value?

o How does it compare to the competitors?

o What have you tried to do to improve this margin?

- **Overhead expenses?**

  o Are they appropriate for your model?

  o How much will they be reduced by the end of the first year when you have more scale?

  o Have you been creative in minimizing these costs?

  o Are you outsourcing the non-essentials for now?

  o Are you keeping fixed costs to a minimum?

  o Are you developing a virtual network?

- **Operating Margins**

  o What will be your starting Operating Margin?

  o What will be at the end of the year?

  o Will you be making money in the 12th month?

  o If not, revisit your model.

- Use the equivalent of the Starbucks' graph (*See Page 216 in Discover The Entrepreneur Within*) to examine every element of your cost structure:

- Did you find new ways to reduce your costs and improve your profitability?

Terrific. You are making great progress. Take a break before you dive into figuring out how much money you will need to get started.

Additional Notes

Chapter 18

HOW MUCH MONEY WILL YOU NEED?

"Money isn't everything...but it ranks right up there with oxygen."- Rita Davenport

"Happiness is a positive cash flow." - Fred Adler

"Anyone who says money can't buy happiness just doesn't know where to shop." - Unknown

~~~~~~~~

Key Topics in this Chapter

- Jane & Bob's "Almost Real Jewelry" Company

- Assumptions & Spreadsheet

- Breakeven

- Money Needed

- Assignment: How much money will you need?

You have developed your financial statements and have a good understanding of cash flow. Now it is time to put everything together and calculate when your business will break-even and how much money you will need to get off the ground. We have created a simple example that we thought you might find helpful. Meet Jane and Bob, two imaginary students of mine. They are trying to launch and test the market for their business in Evanston, IL. Being a test market, these numbers may be a bit small for your taste, but the thought process is exactly the same for a much larger business.

Almost Real Jewelry

Jane and Bob (J&B) want to launch a jewelry company adjacent to their college campus in downtown Evanston. Their intent is to try this out for a year or two in this location, refine the concept and then scale up to other campuses.

As students, they know that their peers love to look snazzy for a night on the town every once and a while. They like to wear jewelry but cannot afford real gold and diamonds as yet. The solution to this problem is *Almost Real Jewelry* - jewelry that looks amazingly real, but costs just a pittance.

Their friends, family and mentors have all asked: How much money will you need? To answer this question, they have developed a spreadsheet, listed all their assumptions and filled in the data so that they can come up with the answers.

Assumptions and Spreadsheet

Location and Supplier: The plan is to rent a small retail store in downtown Evanston where student traffic is very high. They assume that it will take them about 3 months to get the store ready for opening. They have lined up a large distributor out of New York to supply the jewelry.

Capital ($000)

Months	1	2	3	4	5	6	7	8	9	10	11	12	TOTAL YR.
Fixed Investments	-3	-5	-2										**-10**
Working Capital			-4										**-4**

Fixed Capital: They have done rough calculations and estimate spending $10,000, all in the first three months, to set up the store and to buy a cash register and a computer.

Working Capital: They will need money to fund the receivables since a large part of the sales will be paid for with credit cards. They will also need to finance the inventory. Normally the distributor in New York would give them 30 days to pay for the merchandize, but since they are a new venture, he wants cash on delivery for at least the first year. After thinking about it, J&B decide to set aside $4,000 for working capital in month 3, just before they open up the store.

Revenues & Gross Margin ($000)

Months	1	2	3	4	5	6	7	8	9	10	11	12	TOTAL YR.
Revenue				3	3	3	4.5	4.5	4.5	6	6	6	**40.5**
Cost of Goods (40%)				-1.2	-1.2	-1.2	-1.8	-1.8	-1.8	-2.4	-2.4	-2.4	**-16.2**
Gross Profit				1.8	1.8	1.8	2.7	2.7	2.7	3.6	3.6	3.6	**24.3**

Sales Estimate: They estimate selling jewelry worth $3,000 / month for the first three months, increasing to $4,500 / month the following quarter and then increasing to $6,000 / month in the final quarter.

Cost of Goods: The cost of goods for the jewelry is 40%, meaning that an item retailing for $50, will cost them $20.

Gross Profit: The gross margin of 60% results in a gross profit of $1,800 / month at the start. It increases to $3,600 / month later on in the year.

Operating Expenses ($000)

Months	1	2	3	4	5	6	7	8	9	10	11	12	TOTAL YR.
Rent				-1	-1	-1	-1	-1	-1	-1	-1	-1	-9
Utilties				-0.3	-0.3	-0.3	-0.3	-0.3	-0.3	-0.3	-0.3	-0.3	-2.7
Sales Expense				-0.5	-0.5	-0.5	-0.5	-0.5	-0.5	-0.5	-0.5	-0.5	-4.5
Admin Expense				-1	-1	-1	-1	-1	-1	-1	-1	-1	-9
Total Operating Expense				**-2.8**	**-2.8**	**-2.8**	**-2.8**	**-2.8**	**-2.8**	**-2.8**	**-2.8**	**-2.8**	**-25.2**

Rent: Despite their best efforts to get a month to month lease, the landlord has insisted on a 12-month lease for $1,000 / month.

Utilities: Are estimated to be $300 / month.

Sales Expense: Jane and Bob plan to work in the store most of the time, but they will need coverage when they are in class. They estimate they can get part time help for $500 / month.

Administration Expense: There are quite a few other expenses - web site hosting, Google AdWords and clicks and other miscellaneous costs. To be on the safe side, they assume $1,000 / month.

On the next page we have combined all these projections. Let's examine how they all come together. To simplify the numbers, taxes and depreciation have been ignored.

Total Cash Flow ($000)

Months	1	2	3	4	5	6	7	8	9	10	11	12	TOTAL YR.
Fixed Investments	-3	-5	-2										-10
Working Capital			-4										-4
Revenue				3	3	3	4.5	4.5	4.5	6	6	6	40.5
Cost of Goods (40%)				-1.2	-1.2	-1.2	-1.8	-1.8	-1.8	-2.4	-2.4	-2.4	-16.2
Gross Profit				1.8	1.8	1.8	2.7	2.7	2.7	3.6	3.6	3.6	24.3
Operating Expenses													
Rent				-1	-1	-1	-1	-1	-1	-1	-1	-1	-9
Utilties				-0.3	-0.3	-0.3	-0.3	-0.3	-0.3	-0.3	-0.3	-0.3	-2.7
Sales Expense				-0.5	-0.5	-0.5	-0.5	-0.5	-0.5	-0.5	-0.5	-0.5	-4.5
Admin Expense				-1	-1	-1	-1	-1	-1	-1	-1	-1	-9
Total Operating Expense				-2.8	-2.8	-2.8	-2.8	-2.8	-2.8	-2.8	-2.8	-2.8	-25.2
OPERATING INCOME				-1	-1	-1	-0.1	-0.1	-0.1	0.8	0.8	0.8	-0.9
CASH FLOW	-3	-5	-6	-1	-1	-1	-0.1	-0.1	-0.1	0.8	0.8	0.8	-14.9
CUMULATIVE CASH FLOW	-3	-8	-14	-15	-16	-17	-17.1	-17.2	-17.3	-16.5	-15.7	-14.9	

Cash Flow

As the business becomes bigger, there will be more complications like depreciation and taxes. For now, let's use a simple model. First let's calculate the cash flow by month. Then, in the next row, we will calculate the cumulative cash flow, which is a running tally of all the cash that has gone out or come in to date (just like your checkbook).

You can see that the cash outflow is ($3,000) in the first month, ($5,000) in the second month and ($6,000) in the third month. At the end of three months, *Almost Real Jewelry* has a negative cash flow of ($14,000). In month four, revenues start to come in, but the expenses still exceed the gross profit and this deficit continues till month 10, when the operating income finally turns positive.

For the total year, the cash flow is a negative ($14,900).

Break-Even

When a business stops losing money, it has reached the magical destination called *break-even*. Two answers interest us. When will this happen and what sales level needs to be achieved for this to occur?

From the spreadsheet we see that *the business starts to break-even in month 10*, when the monthly cash flow turns positive.

What are the break-even sales? We know the answer is somewhere between $4,500 / month (sales in month nine when the business still loses money) and $6,000 / month (when it starts to make money).

The exact formula to calculate breakeven sales is: operating expenses / gross margin %.

$$\$2800 / 60\% = \$4,667$$

Almost Real Jewelry needs $4,667 / month of sales to break-even and this is forecasted to occur in the tenth month of operating the business.

Money Needed

How much money will *Almost Real Jewelry* need to start this business? For that, you need to look at the *largest negative number* in the cumulative cash flow. This occurs at the end of month nine and amounts to ($17,300). This, then, is the minimum amount that J&B should line up before getting started. However, things rarely go as planned, so you should assume that you will need more money than this.

One way to look at the risk involved is to do a sensitivity analysis. Look at the cash flow and see what happens if you start a month later, because of some snafu due to the landlord or the distributor; or what happens if sales build up slower than anticipated. It is better to think about these things before you start rather than when you are in the middle of the storm. The worst time to try and raise additional money is when you needed it "yesterday." Smart entrepreneurs do not take unnecessary risks.

The reality is that everything always costs more than you anticipate, sales ramp up more slowly than desired and unexpected things always seem to happen at the last moment. I suggest having a minimum safety factor of 25%, which means that Jane and Bob should line up at least $22,000 before they get started. $25,000 would be even better.

"Nothing is more imminent than the impossible.... What we must always foresee is the unforeseen." - Victor Hugo, Les Miserables

Assignment: Money Needed

Use this template to determine how much money you will need. Feel free to change the categories to meet your situation.

Cash Flow ($000)

Months	1	2	3	4	5	6	7	8	9	10	11	12	TOTAL YR.
Fixed Investments													
Working Capital													
Revenue													
Cost of Goods (40%)													
Gross Profit													
Operating Expenses													
Rent													
Utilties													
Sales Expense													
Admin Expense													
Total Operating Expense													
OPERATING INCOME													
CASH FLOW													
CUMULATIVE CASH FLOW													

Breakeven Sales Rate? Calculation: Operating Expenses / Gross Margin %	$
Business Breaks Even in Month:	months
Maximum Negative Cash Flow is:	$
25% of above number for contingencies =	$
Total Money Needed (add the two numbers above)	$

Additional Notes

Chapter 19

OPERATIONS PLAN

"Plans are nothing; planning is everything." - *Dwight Eisenhower*

"Many people spend more time in planning the wedding than they do in planning the marriage." - *Zig Ziglar*

"It is not the strongest of the species that survive, not the most intelligent, but the one most responsive to change." - *Charles Darwin*

~~~~~~~~

Key Topics in this Chapter

- Key Components of the Operations Plan

- Supporting data checklist

- Where to next?

You have learned how to construct financial statements, understood the importance of cash flow and examined every element of cost in your business. You have reviewed your business model and perhaps pivoted once, twice, maybe more. Good for you. Now it is time to put your latest thinking on paper.

Key Components of the Operations Plan

You will recall that the final business plan will be 10 pages while the pitch with the same focus will be 10 slides. The first half of the plan was completed when you worked on the Marketing plan. Now it is time to do the second half of this exercise.

1. **Problem / Solution**
2. **Product**
3. **Customer**
4. **Competition**
5. **Marketing & Sales**
6. **Business Model**
7. **Financial Plan**
8. **Funding**
9. **Team**
10. **Timeline**

 **Operations Plans**

There is nothing here that you have not worked on or thought about. Use the supporting data checklist to ensure that you have thought about all these things to ensure that you have a solid operating plan.

Assignment: Develop your Operations Plan
Use this Supporting Data Checklist to Complete It

As before, these checklists are designed to help you marshal your thoughts. Yes, the questions are repetitive, but the answers do change over time, so update what you have done. A bit more work now, may save you a lot of heartburn later.

6. Business Model:

☐ *Making Money: Do you know how you will do this?*

☐ *Pricing: Is it appropriate for the value you are providing?*

☐ *Cost of Goods: Can it be reduced?*

☐ *Overhead Expenses: Have you deferred all non-essential costs? Made as many costs variable as possible? Do you have the necessary structure to provide the service required by your model?*

☐ *Do you have the right analogs and antilogs?*

☐ *7. Financial Plans:*

    ☐ *Updated P&L by month for Year 1*

    ☐ *Updated Balance Sheet by Quarter for Year 1.*

☐ *8. Funds Needed:*

    ☐ *Breakeven Sales Volume:*

    ☐ *Breakeven Sales Month:*

    ☐ *Maximum Negative Cash Flow:*

    ☐ *How much funding are you planning for? (Suggested Funding: 125% to 150% of maximum negative cash flow):*

    ☐ *Thoughts on how, and from whom, you will raise this money*

    ☐ *Concerns and doubts*

☐ *9. The Team*

☐ *Brief description of every member of your team:*

☐ *Is this a strong team? Why?*

☐ *Do you have a Team Charter? How satisfied are you with it?*

☐ *Have you benchmarked yourself against your charter?*

☐ *Why should anyone invest in this team?*

☐ *Are there any positions you will need to fill in the near future?*

☐ **10. Timeline**

    ☐ *Lay out your timeline for the major events (distribution, investment, sales) by month for Year 1.*

    ☐ *Lay out your timeline for the major events by quarter for Years 2 & 3.*

Where to Next?

You have done all the necessary work to write your business plan and develop your slide deck to pitch your business to anyone. How do you feel? Relieved because you made it this far, but nervous perhaps anticipating what lies ahead? Take a moment to reflect how far you have come. You are close to launch!

If you have not already done so, it's time to take the journey within, starting with the next chapter. Entrepreneurship is a long journey - it's a way of life - a choice you must make. It is worth looking within and calibrating your compass as you head off in search of your Shangri-La.

"I think you travel to search and you come back home to find yourself there." - *Chimamanda Ngozi Adichie*

Additional Notes

PART IV

LOOKING WITHIN

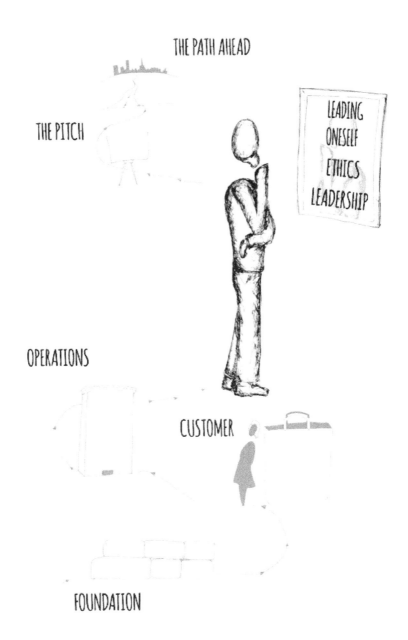

This may be the most important section of the book. You will understand what leadership really is, whether leaders are born and how to become an effective leader. Then you will examine whether ethics are a hindrance to success or a cornerstone of a well-lived life. Finally, you will look at the tools for leading yourself: a moral compass, values, principles and a code of conduct. You will learn how to achieve flow and perhaps even bliss in your life. The journey within requires much - the time to start is now.

Chapter 20

LEADERSHIP

"People ask the difference between a leader and a boss. The leader leads, and the boss drives." – *Theodore Roosevelt*

"A leader is best when people barely know he exists, when his work is done, his aim fulfilled, they will say: we did it ourselves." – *Lao Tzu*

"Leadership is the capacity to translate vision into reality." – *Walter Bennis*

~~~~~~~~

Key Topics in this Chapter

- What is leadership?

- Leaders and Misleaders

- Effective leadership

- Leadership versus Management

- How best to effect change?

- Are leaders born?

- Assignment: What kind of a leader are you today?

As an entrepreneur, you will have to lead others. You will also need to learn to lead yourself.

What makes a leader? Words such as visionary, charismatic, empowering, demanding, articulate and even good looking are often offered as a definition. Are these not just mere traits? Does simply having these qualities make you a leader?

I am told that the greatest challenge faced in leading people is the difficulty in aligning people towards a common goal to achieve results. People wonder whether leadership is something one is born with and whether they have this magical "gift."

Let's explore answers to these questions.

What Is Leadership?

Does running a company make you a leader? How about heading up an NGO or a non-profit whose cause you deeply believe in? What about the Davos crowd? They are rich, well known, have many titles - they must surely be leaders. But are they?

The answer can be found in eliminating what leadership is not. James M. Burns[28] in his book *Leadership* offers the following:

> *"Many acts heralded...as instances of leadership... acts of oratory, manipulation, sheer self-advancement, brute coercion – are not such."*

> *"Much of what commonly passes off as leadership – conspicuous position-taking without followers or follow-through, posturing on various public stages, ... authoritarianism – is no more leadership than...small boys...who continue to strut along...after the procession has turned a side street...."*

The talking heads on TV are not leaders. Being famous, rich, handsome and declaiming upon a popular cause does not confer leadership either. It is true that you may have to listen to your boss at work, but does that make your boss a leader? No, because leadership is not defined by a title.

> *"The only definition of a leader is someone who has followers. Some are prophets others thinkers. But without followers there can be no leader." - Peter Drucker*

It is the presence of followers then that is the defining feature. Buddha, Christ and Aristotle have been dead for two millennia, but people still follow them and are influenced by their teachings. They offered a vision, a goal. They taught ways to achieve these goals. We still study them, we learn from them and we follow their teachings. That is leadership.

Leaders and Misleaders

Lincoln had followers, as did Churchill, Gandhi, MLK and Mandela. But so did Mao Zedong, Stalin, Mussolini, Hitler and Jim Jones of Guyana infamy.

The first group is generally revered for its leadership. On the other hand, under the leadership of Mao and Stalin millions died of starvation. Hitler tried to eliminate an entire race of people. Jim Jones got his followers to drink poisoned Kool-Aid. However, every one of these people had followers. By our definition, we must conclude that they were all leaders.

---

[28] Burns, James MacGregor. *Leadership*. New York. HarperCollins, 1978.

Is there then no difference between good and evil, between right and wrong, in leadership? I believe there is and will address this in the next chapter. Peter Drucker sidestepped this argument elegantly by characterizing them as leaders and misleaders.

Some leaders lead, others mislead. Leaders create *change,* sometimes for the better and sometimes for the worse. Leadership does not come with any guarantee of betterment, only of change, which may lift lives or destroy them.

Effective Leadership

"An effective leader is not someone who is loved or admired. He is someone whose followers do the right things…. Leadership is not rank, privileges, titles, or money. It is responsibility." - Peter Drucker

We spend much of our lives trying to get people to like us, maybe even love or admire us. We equate an admiring throng of people with a successful life. But deep within us, we know this is not the case. In fact, leadership is a very different journey, one of serving others, taking responsibility and making the tough decisions that may sometimes result in vilification. One of my students wonderfully defined leadership as having "the capacity for aloneness."

Leadership is not about the crowds, although followers are necessary. It is about the willingness and ability to lead, regardless of popularity or circumstances. To do what is right and to do what needs to be done. It demands a focus on a mission that is greater than one's personal glory and aggrandizement. Saying "No" may be the greatest act of leadership.

Some years back, Jim Collins studied companies that had gone from being mediocre to great in his mega bestseller *Good to Great.* One of the key factors effecting this transformation was the presence of a certain kind of leader that he dubbed a "Level 5 leader." These leaders were capable and had ambition but their ambition was first and foremost for the company or cause, not for themselves.

Even more surprising perhaps was the finding that these leaders had great humility. When things went well, they gave the credit to their people and when things went wrong, they looked in the mirror. They were not driven by titles or money. They were more "plow horses than show horses."

Do such people really exist and if so, how come we don't hear about them? The simple reason is that they do not seek publicity or adulation for themselves. They don't look for approval. Look at winning teams or students that consistently do well in a certain class. Examine organizations where things work well but there appears to be no leader in sight. There is most likely a Level 5 leader in the background. Sometimes they do become famous but they still deflect the glory. John Wooden, the UCLA coach, who won many basketball championships, but never sought praise for himself, was one such leader.

Leadership versus Management

Professor John Kotter[29] in *A Force For Change* explained that while Leadership is about *change,* Management is about *control.* (The chart below is derived from his book.) Both deal with the same factors of: creating an agenda, people, execution and results. However, they do so with different time horizons in mind, which result in different actions and behaviors.

Management focuses on getting things done *now,* delivering results *this quarter,* dealing with people's issues *today.*

Leadership looks at the long term with a goal to create far-reaching results. This divergence in time horizon and focus often creates havoc in the process.

---

[29] Kotter, John. *A Force For Change.* New York: Free Press, 1990.

	MANAGEMENT	LEADERSHIP
Creating Agenda	Planning & Budgeting	Establishing Direction, Vision
Developing People	Organizing & Staffing	Aligning People
Execution	Controlling & Problem Solving	Motivating, Energizing, Inspiring
Outcome	Predictability & Profitability	Change, often Dramatic

CONTROL   **CHANGE**

Which of these two is more important? Yes, it is a trick question. They are both needed to achieve the goals. It is said that management without leadership results in stagnation, while leadership without management leads to chaos. It is the balance of the two that leads to a healthy organization and positive outcomes.

"Management is doing things right; leadership is doing the right things." – Peter Drucker

How Best To Effect Change?

Assume you have just taken over an organization in disarray. The vision is not clear, the people do not like each other, often work at cross-purposes and the results are abysmal. Now what?

Most organizations follow a process similar to what Professor John Kotter suggested in *A Force For Change*, which is to:

1. Establish a new direction based on an in-depth analysis.
2. Align people with unwavering commitment to a Vision.
3. Motivate, inspire and energize people.

I have seen this process unfold many times in America. A new CEO comes in and decides he needs to change everything. He hires a big consulting company to do a business analysis. He and his team go off on a retreat to think about the future direction of the company, and after some discussion arrive at a new vision and strategy. This is then rolled out across the company with new programs created to motivate, inspire and energize the rank and file.

My experience is that such efforts generally fail. Oh, the new plan works for a short while but the change and acceptance is not deep rooted. The consultants leave, the playbook is relegated to some shelf to gather dust, the leader gets a new assignment and life resumes its previous rhythm. Until, of course, another new leader appears who decides it is time to be "inspired" again.

Jim Collins[30] offered a different approach in *Good to Great*, which I think has greater merit.

- *First pick the people, then the strategy.* No one person is ever good enough to figure out the right strategy. A good team is needed.
- *Get the right people on the bus.* Choose people who really want to be there, those who are a cultural fit and have the needed skills.

---

[30] Collins, Jim. *Good to Great.* New York: HarperBusiness, 2001.

- *Get the wrong people off the bus.* This group includes: whiners, credit hogs, "it's all about me" people and those who do not keep their commitments. It is not possible to work around them. Their presence and involvement is cancerous.
- *Develop a hedgehog concept.* The hedgehog knows only *one* thing. Similarly, a company can be really good at only *one* thing. Figure out what you can be the best at in the world while making money and focus on this to the exclusion of everything else.
- *Culture of Discipline.* A to-do list is important but a not to-do list is even more important. Everyone is doing too much and much of it is not productive. Simplify, simplify, simplify.

To lead a company, you do not have to go to a fancy resort, hire pricey consultants and bring back a new vision. The Level 5 leaders did not succeed because of brilliant strategy, or because the industry trends were favorable, or because they went and preached the gospel of culture and oneness. No. They, along with their team, figured out what needed to be done, put their noses to the grindstone and got it done.

Focus on substance, involve people, be humble, give credit to others, get out of the way and then watch people succeed.

Are Leaders Born?

Many times students, or clients, share with me their doubts as to whether they have what it takes to be a leader. They feel they lack key attributes such as oratory, charisma and likeability. They believe that some people are born leaders and they are not part of that select group.

Are leaders really born? Professor John Kotter suggests that there are four hereditary factors: *Drive, Intelligence, Emotional Intelligence* and *Integrity.* He further believes that very few people have all four factors.

Peter Drucker felt otherwise: *"There may be 'born leaders,' but too few to depend on them. Leadership must be learned — and can be learned."*

How does one learn these skills? How does one prepare to become a leader? John Kotter suggests seeking challenging assignments that broaden you. Look at both good and bad leaders around you and pick your right role models. Jim Collins suggests focusing consciously on personal development, self-reflection and seeking mentors and great teachers. John Maxwell exhorts that the *"quickest way to get leadership: solve problems!"*

You need both outer and inner development with the latter being more important. We will discuss this further in upcoming chapters.

The best time to get started is now. Remember Lincoln failed at virtually everything till he was 40. Then he saved a country!

Assignment: Take a Personal Inventory

Answer these questions as you see things today.

1. **What is your definition of leadership today?**

2. **On the management / leadership spectrum, where would you place yourself? Why?**

3. **What do you believe are the key skills needed for leadership?**

4. **Which ones do you have and which ones do you need to work on?**

5. How self-aware are you? And what can you do to become more self-aware?

6. What life experiences have you had that have made you who you are?

7. How would you evaluate yourself as a leader today?

Chapter 21

THE ROLE OF ETHICS

"It is curious - curious that physical courage should be so common in the world, and moral courage so rare." - Mark Twain

"Have the courage to say no. Have the courage to face the truth. Do the right thing because it is right. These are the magic keys to living your life with integrity." - Clement Stone

"If you don't have integrity, you have nothing. You can't buy it. You can have all the money in the world, but if you are not a moral and ethical person, you really have nothing." - Henry Kravis

~~~~~~~~

Key Topics in this Chapter

- What are Ethics?

- Ethics: Hindrance or Foundation?

- Are Ethics Subjective?

- Good and Evil leaders: Three Key Differentiators

- 100% of the Time is Easier

- Assignment: Reflections

From an early age children are inculcated with the notions of right and wrong by parents and society. With the passing years, these ideas become quaint and are often buried within us. When I ask my students, clients and friends, how many of them witness cheating and lying in their day-to-day environment, sadly nearly everybody nods. This occurs despite clear codes of conduct in colleges and in the workplace. Young people, looking at the world, may conclude that ethics are not needed in life. Some may even see ethics as a hindrance to success. In self-reflective moments though, most human beings realize that ethics are the foundation of a well-lived life.

What Are Ethics?

The word *ethics* is derived from the Greek word "ethos" which deals with good and bad, moral duty, or a set of moral principles and values. For our purpose let us define this term as a guiding philosophy for our lives.

It turns out that Ethics is mostly a study of *"right vs. right" decisions and not "right vs. wrong" decisions,* as is usually thought. Amoral people are rare. The vast majority of the people clearly know right from wrong. This is why the study of ethics focuses mainly on how to make decisions between two right choices.

Let's take an example. A mother with small children is debating whether she should go back to work. The children need her attention at this age. On the other hand, the extra income from the job would allow the family to send the children to a better school. Working or staying at home with the children are both *right* choices. It is these kind of dilemmas that are the provenance of ethics. Philosophers have developed models for these paradigms, including "Utilitarian" – doing what is right for the most people, and "The Golden Rule" – doing unto others as we would want done to us.

The following dialogue appears in Rushworth Kidder's book[31]:

Question: "What is it about those situations that strike us as ethical conundrums and resist every effort to fit themselves into the paradigm?"

Answer: "Usually there is a simple reason they do not fit: They turn out to be right-versus-wrong issues."

What does he mean by this? Simply, our struggle with a right versus wrong decision is not because the answer is difficult, but because we do not like the answer. We want to find a way out, figure out an exception or rationalize our action. The answer in essence is easy, while the resulting action may be hard.

Ethics: Hindrance or Foundation?

If one reads the headlines, cheating and lying seem common.
"Lying, cheating, violence - all ingredients for success, teen survey says…. 71% say they feel fully prepared to make ethical decisions when they enter the workforce…. Yet 38%…believe it is sometimes necessary to cheat, plagiarize, lie or even behave violently in order to succeed." - DenverPost.com 12/5/07

"Stanford University investigating 'unusually high' number of cheaters" - New York Daily News, 3/28/15

"Nearly half of the school's (Harvard) incoming freshmen admitted to cheating on homework, exams or other assignments…. The elite institution is still reeling from a 2012 cheating scandal in which dozens of kids swapped and plagiarized answers during a course called 'Introduction to Congress'." - New York Post 9/6/13

---

[31] *How Good People Make Tough Choices"* by Rushworth Kidder. See Bibliography.

I have lived most of my life in Illinois where politicians, especially governors, go to jail with frightening regularity. In the business world the list is also long: Enron, Bernie Madoff, World Bank, Tyco, just to name a few. These examples are all from the US, a relatively honest country to do business in according to Transparency International[32]. One can only smile ruefully in observing Groucho Marx's acerbic comment:

"Those are my principles, and if you don't like them... well, I have others."

Does everyone really cheat? More importantly, should you cheat? Yes, there is temptation all around. Since time immemorial the sages have exhorted us to "Know thyself." Why? So we can look within ourselves to understand the purpose of life and to determine our code of conduct, behavior and values.

We must make the choice. Will we chase riches, power and fame at any cost? Will we choose the truth or employ it situationally thereby embracing a "drowsy morality[33]?" Or will we define a "rich life" differently, one that embraces a higher purpose and conduct in life?

Lord John Fletcher Moulton, an English mathematician and lawyer, in a seminal essay[34] in 1927 defined ethics as the *"obedience to the unenforceable."* He further added: *"The real greatness of a nation, it's true civilization, is measured by the extent of this land of obedience to the unenforceable…The true test is the extent to which the individuals composing the nation can be trusted to obey self-imposed law."*

I believe character is the foundation of a good leader or a good human being. *Ethics, including integrity,* is the foundation of character. We must always be honest with ourselves and face reality rather than merely rationalize our actions. In the United States, most businesses you will encounter will be honest. Most people you will deal with will be honest. But even when you come across dishonesty and the temptation to join in presents itself, you must remember that this is your life, your canvas and your painting. What will you paint on your canvas? How will you live your life?

Are Ethics Subjective?

In discussions about right and wrong, people often seek shelter in the argument that ethics are subjective and situational. It turns out that in virtually every country, people know the difference between right and wrong. Lying, cheating and murder are considered unethical just about everywhere. It is true that the conditions and circumstances often lead to the abandonment of these principles. *However, the prevalence of a practice does not mean that people do not know right from wrong.*

Recently, *Reader's digest* [35] did an interesting global social experiment. It visited 16 cities and dropped 12 wallets in every city. Each wallet contained approximately $50 in local currency, a business card, some photographs and a cell number. **47% of these wallets were returned.** Below is a sampling of the results:

---

[32] The US is ranked #19 out of 175 countries on the 2014 Perception Corruption Index done by Transparency International.
[33] David Miller, PhD
[34] "Law and Manner, " The Atlantic, 1927, by Lord John Fletcher Moulton
[35] "Most Honest Cities: *Reader's digest* "Lost Wallet" Test, Reader's Digest 2015

City	Number of wallets returned out of 12	Comment made by person returning wallet
Helsinki	11	"Of course we returned the wallet. Honesty is an inner conviction."
Mumbai	9	"My conscience wouldn't let me do anything wrong."
New York, Budapest	8	"I flipped through all the papers and saw the family photo and thought, Aw, he has two kids. We have to give this back."
Moscow, Amsterdam	7	"I am convinced that people should help one another and if I can make someone a little happier, I will."
Berlin, Ljubljana	6	"My parents taught me how important being honest is. Once I lost an entire bag, but I got everything back. So, I know what it feels like."
London, Warsaw	5	"There were those who advised me not to bother looking for the owner," she said. "But I thought that someone might badly need that money."
Rio de Janeiro, Bucharest, Zurich	4	"In my teens, I picked up a magazine in a department store and left without paying. When my mother found out, she told me this behavior was unacceptable."
Prague	3	"It's something you simply should do naturally."
Madrid	2	"I couldn't keep a purse that wasn't mine."
Lisbon	1	People returning the wallet were from another country.

While this is not a statistical sample, it does provide a window into the world. Sadly, only about half the wallets were returned. Interestingly there seemed to be no correlation between a country's wealth and honesty. While our culture and surroundings do affect us, ethics is ultimately a very personal journey. It is a choice we, and we alone, must make.

"Relativity applies to physics, not ethics." - *Albert Einstein*

Good and Evil leaders: Three Key Differentiators

Over the years my students and I have been studying good and evil leaders. Each year the students make presentations on eight leaders choosing both world and business leaders. Furthermore, half of these leaders are generally considered to be good and the other half, bad or evil. The students have the right to change the classification if they so choose. Some of the people we have studied are:

World Leaders: Lincoln, Jefferson, Gandhi, MLK, Mandela, Thatcher, Hitler, Stalin, Mussolini, Mao, Pol Pot and Castro.

National / Business Leaders: Sam Walton, Herb Kelleher, Bill Gates, Steve Jobs, Jack Welch, Jeff Skilling, Martha Stewart, Al Dunlap, Jimmy Hoffa, Rod Blagojevich and Jim Jones.

The students research these leaders in some depth and present their findings to the class. While the data is not statistically significant, it is informative. I also ask them to rate the leaders on the following factors:

Personal Attributes	External Attributes	Process
Integrity	Focus on self or cause	Quality of people on team
Determination	Vision	Ability to face facts
Attitude	Results orientation	Culture
Intelligence	Communicator	Clarity of goals
Emotional Intelligence	Charisma	Ability to execute

Most leaders share many of the qualities listed above. They are leaders, after all, and these are the attributes that make people leaders. However, the most interesting insights are found **in the qualities where they differ.**
Over the years, I have consistently found these three key differentiators.

1. *Character*: Very simply, good leaders have good character and integrity. The bad leaders lie blatantly. While they may be "strong characters," their character is poor. According to author David McCullough *"Character is the single most important asset of a president."* It is indeed that simple.
2. *Where is the focus?* Is it on something bigger than "me?" or is it just on "me"? Lincoln's focus was on "The Union Must Survive" while Mao's and Stalin's focus was on total control over everyone and everything. Don't be fooled by the rhetoric that is often associated with these "revolutionaries." Behind most of them lie gargantuan egos devoid of any self-reflection. Learn to separate propaganda from reality.
3. *People:* Good leaders surround themselves with strong independent thinkers who are willing to speak up and challenge them when needed. The misleaders, the dictators, the delusional, surround themselves with thugs and enforcers.

These same differentiators can be used to evaluate people and companies you encounter going forward. When in doubt, ask these two questions: *Would I follow this leader? Do I really want to work with this person?*

100% of the Time is Easier

"How Will You Measure Your Life?" by Harvard Professor Clayton Christensen[36], has only three sections: Happiness in Career, Happiness in Relationships and Staying out of Jail. The last one always elicits a chuckle, but it is the most important chapter of all. Jeff Skilling, of Enron fame, was a classmate of Christensen at the Harvard Business School and considered to be the smartest person in the class. Mr. Christensen points out that no one plans to be a cheat or make a career as a crook. But life happens, events occur and without an ethical compass, it is easy to get lost.

He suggests that telling the truth 100% of the time is much easier than 98% of the time. You do not have to remember what you said to whom, for there is only one version of one story. The bigger problem is that lying occasionally is a slippery slope. Once you get started where do you stop?

Many people bristle at the notion of telling the truth 100% of the time. They want some wiggle room. After all, their circumstances are unique. Besides how can one commit to a course of action without knowing what lies ahead? But that is exactly the point of having an ethical compass. It is there to guide us in unchartered waters.

Is it possible that we will fail at times when events overwhelm us? Yes. But then we should pick ourselves up, look at the truth and do what is needed. This is a different approach than one where you say: "Let's see what happens and if I can be honest, I will try to be honest."

---

[36] Christensen, Clayton. *How will you measure your life?* New York: HarperBusiness, 2012.

"The truth knocks on the door and you say, 'Go away, I'm looking for the truth,' and so it goes away. Puzzling." - Robert Pirsig

Assignment: Reflections

Reflect on the following. Be honest with yourself.

1. How strong is your ethical compass today? Are there areas that you need to look at more closely?

2. Did you ever find a wallet or some other valuable? What did you do? Why?

3. Did someone ever return something that you had lost? How did you feel?

4. Did you ever take or keep something that wasn't yours? How did that feel?

5. Reflect on a right versus right decision that you faced and how you resolved it?

6. How do you approach your life today: Ethics as a hindrance to success or the essence of your life? The only person you need to tell the truth to is yourself.

"The truth is there all the time. Embrace it 100% of the time. It will make for a more fulfilled life." – Verinder Syal

Additional Notes

Additional Notes

Chapter 22

LEADING ONESELF

"People travel to wonder at the height of the mountains, at the huge waves of the seas, at the long course of the rivers, at the vast compass of the ocean, at the circular motion of the stars, and yet they pass by themselves without wondering." - St. Augustine

"Control is not leadership; management is not leadership; leadership is leadership. If you seek to lead, invest at least 50% of your time in leading yourself - your own purpose, ethics, principles, motivation, conduct. Invest at least 20% leading those with authority over you and 15% leading your peers." - Dee Hock - Founder and CEO Emeritus, Visa

"The first and best victory is to conquer self." - Plato

~~~~~~~~

Key Topics in this Chapter

- True North

- Code of Conduct

- Voices in our Head: Fear & Success

- Happiness

- Follow Your Bliss

- Assignment: Find Your Flow

Why is leading oneself the hardest journey of all? It involves our feelings, fears, aspirations, hopes and dreams. To look within and see who we are, who we want to be, and what our purpose is, is frightening. It feels like a deep dive into an abyss. However, this may well be the most important journey of all.

TRUE NORTH

"True North is the internal compass that guides you successfully through life…. It is your orienting point – your fixed point in a spinning world – that helps you stay on track as a leader." – Bill George[37], True North – Discover Your Authentic Leadership

We need a compass to navigate the inevitable vicissitudes of life. Bill George believes that we cannot live anyone else's life or copy their leadership style. Rather, we must be our own authentic selves. The key components of this compass are *Self-Awareness*, *Values* and *Motivations*.

Self-Awareness

How does one start this inner journey of self-discovery? By slowing down and taking the time to reflect on who we are, what makes us tick, where we want to go and why? As St. Augustine lamented, we do everything but this. If anything, technology has exacerbated this attention deficit even further.

Develop a routine to take time for yourself everyday. This is not being selfish. It is necessary for being well and balanced and at peace with the world. Try meditating, exercising, listening to music, dancing, going to church - any activity that allows you to turn off your brain is a good place to start.

My students have found the *Peeling the Onion* self-awareness exercise from *True North* very helpful. I know it will help you too. Please do this now.

- *The Exercise*:
    - On a scale of 1-10, with "10" being high and "1" being low, score yourself on several questions which are detailed below. This should take about five minutes.
    - Then send this questionnaire – a spreadsheet works well – to ten of your family members, friends and colleagues, and ask them to rate you.
    - Average those ten answers and compare them to the score you gave yourself for each question.

---

[37] George, Bill. *True North*. San Francisco: Jossey-Bass, 2007.

Answers on a scale of 1-10. 1=Poor; 10= Excellent	Your Rating	Average of 10 outside answers
1. How self-confident am I?		
2. How aware am I of my moods and emotions?		
3. How effective am I in regulating my moods to minimize the impact on other people?		
4. When confronted with situations that are displeasing to me, how well do I take the time to think clearly about them before responding or reacting?		
5. When I receive critical feedback from others, how well am I able to take the feedback and respond in a constructive manner without acting defensively?		
6. How well do I understand the emotional makeup of others and their needs?		
7. How sensitive am I in relating to others' needs and helping them?		
8. How skilled am I in building lasting relationships?		
9. How well do I network with others and create networks of people with common interests?		
10. How effective am I in leading teams?		
11. Do others follow me voluntarily?		
12. How persuasive am I in convincing others of our mutual interests?		

- *Now answer these Questions:*
    - o   How do I see myself and how does that compare to how others see me?

    - o   What things surprised you the most?

    - o   What are my strengths?

    - o   What are my needs?

    - o   What are my blind spots?

o   Where am I vulnerable?

o   How comfortable am I with myself today?

o   Should I make any changes?

I did this survey a few years back along with my students. I thought I knew myself quite well but I learned things I was not aware of, including the fact that my behavior varied depending on whom I was with. It gave me valuable insight into what changes I needed to make to be the person I aspired to be. Some of the answers may surprise you, especially which person says what. That is why taking the average is the best comparison. Do not dwell on any one number. Some people may refuse to fill out the questionnaire. Don't worry, ask other people. Just get the required ten responses.

Values & Principles

Values are things that matter to us. We all have them even though they may not be top of mind. Part of becoming more self-aware is to be more in touch with these values. What are your values? Perhaps the list below will jog your mind.

Authentic	Compassion	Commitment
Integrity	Excellence	Creativity
Kindness	Honesty	Learning
Curiosity	Family	Reflective
Hard work	Helping others	Making a difference

Principles are a set of standards for living and leading that embody our values. If integrity is one of your values, a principle might be "I will always approach all business and personal dealings with total integrity." Develop your principles today and construct your ethical boundaries now.

Extrinsic and Intrinsic Motivations

We all have motivators that are extrinsic in nature: money, power, promotions, titles, prestige, recognition, social status, big houses and fancy cars.

There is nothing wrong with such motivations. They are the fuel that drive our everyday lives. However, this is a race that cannot be won. Someone else will always have a bigger house, a fancier car, grander titles and more money. Chasing these baubles, after a while, will not satisfy you because they cannot fill your inner needs.

Intrinsic motivations are the nourishment for the soul. These include personal growth, challenging jobs, helping others develop, finding meaning, making a difference and being true to yourself.

Understand that you need both. The question is one of emphasis. A greater focus on intrinsic motivations will lead to a richer life, a richness not defined by dollars, but by greater inner satisfaction and peace.

The Need For A Compass

Sure, these are nice things to talk about in a class, but do they really have any applicability in the real world? Perhaps this email from one of my students provides the answer.

"Prof - Good thing we spent a substantial amount of time talking about a moral compass. I can't begin to describe how important this really is once you start working. This past month has been a whirlwind of difficult situations and I am constantly struggling to make sure I don't lose sight of mine. It's been particularly interesting to contemplate how/why my moral compass doesn't always match the moral compass of many of the people I am surrounded by. This hasn't necessarily been a bad thing, just something new and different I've had to deal with...
To say the least, I am continuously learning…. I'm still reflecting on discussions we had and more importantly applying them to everyday situations. What more can you ask from a class?"

Ethical crises do not come with flashing signs and warning lights. They come suddenly with no time to prepare or to seek advice. Living life on your own terms requires you to be prepared for such eventualities. To paraphrase the Buddha: Work on your compass now.

CODE OF CONDUCT

I urge my students to develop a code of conduct for themselves and to look at it often. This is a good way to take the above learnings and convert them to something concrete. To make it usable, I ask them to come up with only five principles. Let's look at some famous codes.

Hippocratic oath: "First do no harm."

United States Military Academy: "A cadet will not lie, cheat, steal, or tolerate those who do."
The Scout Oath:
On my honor, I will do my best,
To do my duty to God and my country and to obey the Scout Law;
To help other people at all times;
To keep myself physically strong, mentally awake and morally straight.

Some of the things that my students come up with are: integrity, commitment, compassion, giving, helping, kindness, taking action, relationships, living a balanced life, no regrets and to stop comparing themselves with others.
Consider developing a code of conduct for yourself.

VOICES IN OUR HEAD:
FEAR & SUCCESS

Fear

There are so many voices in our heads. With social media, the cacophony is even louder. Who we are and what is important to us is hard to figure out. Fear, behind a mask of bravado, is never far away. What are we afraid of? Of not being good enough, not being liked, failing at a job, not having enough money, being alone - the list is endless. We worry about being rejected by others. We mold our actions to fit in with others so as to belong to something. But the fear still does not go away.

It even bleeds into confusion and indecisiveness. Many young people have so many choices that they do not know which way to turn. They are afraid of making a mistake, picking the wrong thing, so they pick nothing. In many ways, they are the *unfortunate* ones. The more fortunate ones do *not* have a choice, so they find a job and get on with their lives. Certainty is never guaranteed; life demands taking chances.

Vincent Van Gogh put it poetically: *"The fishermen know that the sea is dangerous and the storm terrible, but they have never found these dangers sufficient reason for remaining ashore."*

As for failure, the founder of IKEA has this to say: *"Only those who are asleep make no mistakes."*

The only failure is not trying.

Success

What is success? Is it being famous, rich and having an armada of admirers? Or does the one with the most toys wins?

The quick answer always is "No, it is much more than that. Relationships are important. Personal growth is important. Leaving a mark is important." In essence, people say they want to focus on intrinsic motivations. But what is the reality? If you are like most people, the pursuit of extrinsic rewards dwarfs everything else.

The time to focus on what is truly important is *now* regardless of your age. Each day is a new gift. What will you do with it? What will you pursue? What feelings will you create?

Tony De Mello[38], a Jesuit priest, provided this profound insight: *"What kind of feelings come upon you when you're in touch with nature, or when you are absorbed in work that you love? Or when you are conversing with someone you enjoy... Compare these feelings with the feelings you have when you win an argument, or when you win a race, or when you become popular, or when everybody's applauding you. These latter feelings I call worldly feelings; the former...soul feelings. Lots of people gain the world and lose their soul."*

David Brooks, *The New York Times* columnist, in a recent TED talk asked: "Should you live for your resume or your eulogy?" How about neither? Are both of these not the "worldly feelings" that De Mello alludes to? Besides, why do you care what people will think of you after you are gone? Will a building or a street named after you really excite you in the after life? Why not focus on this day and make something wondrous out of it? The moment is now. Seize it.

HAPPINESS

The Constitution of the United States proclaims that people *"... are endowed by their Creator with certain unalienable Rights, that among these are Life, Liberty and the pursuit of Happiness."*

Aristotle emphatically stated: *"Happiness is the meaning and the purpose of life, the whole aim and end of human existence."*

What exactly is happiness and how and where do we find it? The Buddha taught that the elimination of pain - and therefore happiness - came from overcoming attachment and ego. Aristotle thought it was from living a virtuous life, which included having meaningful and deep friendships. Jesus pointed to the grass and the flowers that just seemed to live as examples to emulate.

Joseph Campbell, the great mythologist, explained that The Garden of Eden, or Nirvana, does not lie someplace out there, but it lies within us, here and now. We do not have to wait for happiness. We can have it today. It is not a destination. Rather it is the scenery along the journey of life.

This all sounds wonderful but how do we translate it to our modern lives? Mihaly Csikszentmihalyi[39], a professor from the University of Chicago, in his groundbreaking book *Flow* explained that there are "two different kinds of enjoyment.... One is physical or body pleasure" such as eating or sex. This can be very satisfying but after a while the enjoyment diminishes. But "there is a state many people value even more...it is the state of total immersion in a task that is challenging yet closely matched to one's abilities." This is called "flow."

---

[38] De Mello, Anthony. *Awareness*. New York. Random House, 2011

[39] Csikszentmihalyi, Mihaly. *Flow*. New York: HarperCollins Publishers, 1990

Therein lies the answer for our everyday lives: doing something we are passionate about and one we also have the skills for. I have tried to capture this idea with this mnemonic, which I often use with my students.

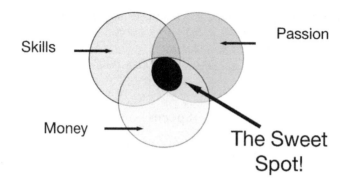

Often the pressures of life - real and perceived - lead us to focus on making money *now* with the intent to come back to our passion and skills at a later stage in life. The longer you wait to do work that you love, the harder it will become. The "Promised Land" will always remain tantalizingly elusive.

Needing to work so as to live is a false dichotomy. What if work were not work but play? What if you loved every minute of it? Would that be a life worth living? Start with work that combines your passion and skills and be in the "flow" now. Making a living may surprisingly become easier.

FOLLOW YOUR BLISS

Joseph Campbell, when asked by students what job or path they should take given that their parents were saying "this" and their friends were saying "that," would always exhort them to "follow your bliss."

Bliss lies beyond happiness. As I think about it, bliss combines "flow" with being your own person, forging your own trail.

Consider this: Henry Thoreau of Walden pond fame who is admired by so many today was considered a failure and a wastrel during his lifetime. But he seemed to have liked, most likely loved, how he lived. Will you dare to do what you love *today* even if so called success may only come a 100 years from now or perhaps never?

Will you follow the herd or choose the "other path" like Spinoza? This other path that is *uncrowded* and where the destination is uncertain. But it holds the possibility to find happiness, or truth, or whatever it is that you seek.

Life is a series of moments. We should strive to have more good moments and fewer bad moments. The best moments come from living up to our greatest human potential, which is when we embrace divinity. They come when we give rather than take, when we do rather than critique, when we love rather than hate and when we embrace today rather than fear tomorrow.

Will you dare to follow your bliss?

***"We must let go of the life we planned, so as to accept the one that is waiting for us." –
Joseph Campbell***

Assignment: Find Your Flow

1. What are your values today? Write out no more than five.

2. What are your extrinsic and intrinsic motivations today?

3. Develop a code of conduct with no more than five principles. Then print it out and post it where you can see it every day.

4. Do you have moments of "Flow?" Describe them.

5. How can you enhance such moments? And, if you have not experienced flow, what do you need to do?

6. What does bliss look like to you?

7. Will you have the courage to follow your bliss?

PART V

THE PITCH

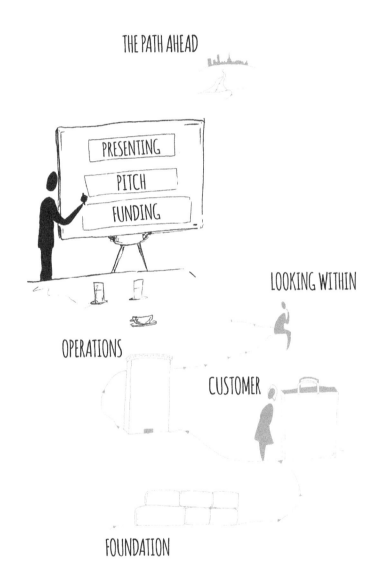

It is time to decide whether you will bootstrap your business or raise outside money. This is a profoundly philosophical decision. You will examine an equitable way to divide the equity pie. Then you will move on to complete your 10-slide pitch deck, 10-page business plan and your one-minute elevator speech. Finally, you will learn how to make a captivating and riveting presentation. It's show time!

Chapter 23

THE FUNDING DECISION

"I am a bootstrapper. I have initiative and insight and guts, but not much money. I will succeed because my efforts and my focus will defeat bigger and better-funded competitors. I am fearless. I keep my focus on growing the business - not on politics, career advancement, or other wasteful distractions." - Seth Godin, The Bootstrapper's Bible

"Money often costs too much." - Ralph Waldo Emerson

"The gods only laugh when people ask them for money." - Japanese proverb

~~~~~~~~

Key Topics in this Chapter

- A Philosophical Decision

- Bootstrapping

- Slicing the Pie

- Raising Outside Money

- Assignment: What is your funding plan?

You know how much money you need to get the business started. The next question to answer is where will this money come from?

A Philosophical Decision

Whether to bootstrap your business or raise outside money is a philosophical decision. As soon as you take in outside money, the dynamics change. You are no longer in full control of the business you built from the ground up. How important is that to you?

It is fashionable today to label oneself a serial entrepreneur. Why are people in a hurry to jump from one thing to another? Is it because they are prolifically creative, or that they have short attention spans and they get bored easily? Why is the next big thing always more enticing?

There is another path. Focus on building a great company, serving customers exceptionally well and helping your people grow. Can you envision being totally passionate about what you are doing and wanting to run to work every day? Only when that task is done would you move on to the next adventure in your life. Why not live this adventure to the fullest first?

Those in a hurry to get to the next big thing, rarely find fulfillment in the moment they are in. Slow down, focus on the current thing, now, with your total attention, capacity, emotion and passion.

My recommendation is to defer raising outside money as long as possible. Use your own resources and build the company you aspire to build in the manner you want to. When the time comes to seek outside money, then by all means do so. But understand that this will change the dynamics of the business, as you start marching to the beat of a different drummer.

"We are our choices." - Jean-Paul Sartre

Bootstrapping

As the name implies, this calls for building your company with your own resources. Perhaps you are lucky and you have such resources. Some of you will quickly conclude that you have no resources.

To challenge this notion of having little or no resources, I want to share with you an exercise that my students have to do. I got this idea from Tina Seelig's *What I wish I knew when I was 20.*

It is called the *$5 / 2 hour* assignment. In the first week of class students form teams with people they have only recently met. Each team is given a sealed envelope with $5. They can take a few days to develop their best idea, but they will have only *2 hours* to execute their idea once they open their envelope. The goal is to make the most money.

The results presented in class a week later range from unimaginative to incredible. Let's see what happened two years ago.

Three teams unquestioningly accepted the perceived constraints of limited resources. They used the five dollars to buy and resell bottled water, coffee and bagels respectively. On average these teams made about $20.

Then things got interesting. Two of the teams decided to utilize their cars using the $5 for gas money. One of them shuttled students to Trader Joe's for a round trip shopping excursion for $5 / person. The other team first tried to ferry students from local bars back to the dormitories late at night, but found no customers. They pivoted and became a limousine service, driving friends, who were now paying customers, to downtown Chicago. These teams made about $50 each.

One team concluded that the 3-minute presentation time in class was the most important asset they had and offered to sell that as advertising time to companies who wanted to recruit on campus. Alas, none of the HR departments of the companies contacted, called them back. They then sold this advertising time to five local restaurants and made a profit of $105.

The final team decided to sell coupons at a discounted rate (think Groupon) for a highly coveted brand of cookies in a creative manner. They donated all the profits to a school charity and raised almost $200.

All the teams were highly motivated with bright students. What, then, accounts for their differing approaches? The difference may lie in a fixed versus growth mindset. The resources that we have are significantly greater than what we imagine them to be. Money is only one of the inputs and often not even the most important ingredient.

"Nothing limits achievement like small thinking; nothing expands possibilities like unleashed imagination." William Arthur Ward

One of my students shared these examples:
- Sophia Amoruso started NastyGal in her garage and bootstrapped it for five years before raising any sort of outside funding.
- Braintree also bootstrapped itself and, instead of using the popular freemium model and it's associated underwriting, generated revenues from the start while keeping costs low. Four years later it was acquired by PayPal.
- TechCrunch and Gawker were both bootstrapped before being bought out by large media groups.

Turn on your imagination and make an inventory of the resources you have. Much greater than you thought, right? Can you bootstrap it for now?

Slicing the Pie

One of the common hurdles that teams face is how to split the pie, i.e., the equity. Let's say that four of you start a business and since you are good friends, you feel that the only fair way to slice the pie is for each of you to own 25% of the company. A few months into it, one of the team members decides to go back to school and another one can now only put in 10 hours a week because things have changed at work. The other two are working day and night and have barely enough time to breathe. The friendship starts to wear thin and the equal split now seems mighty unfair.

My colleague and entrepreneur, Professor Michael Moyer[40], offers a creative answer to this dilemma in his book *Slicing Pie*. Let us examine his key points.

Everything has a value - such as:
- People's work and time.
- Assets, like a computer or printer, which are contributed to the operation.
- Cash that is put into the business.
- With each such activity the value of the business increases. The pie gets bigger.

But everything does not have equal value.
- Certain skills may have a higher price. Coding skills may be of greater value than creating content for a blog, for example.
- And cash, at the outset, may be the most precious contribution of all.

Develop and agree upon a model of relative value. Professor Moyer suggests the following framework:
- Contributions in kind, such as computers, printers, iPads or even a car, create a value of *1X* units. A one-year old computer valued at $500 will create 500 units of value.
- Agree upon the different hourly rates for the different functional skills by looking at the going market rates. For example, you might find that engineers are getting paid $80,000 per year, which translates to

---

[40] Moyer, Mike. *Slicing Pie*. Lake Forest, IL: Lake Shark Ventures, 2012.

$40/hour based on 2000 hours per year. A social media job may be valued at $50,000 per year ($25/hour) while a finance specialist may be $70,000 per year ($35/hour).

- More importantly, if the person's compensation is deferred, then the unit multiplier is *2X*. After all, saving cash is very important at this stage.
- If someone donates hard cash, the units are created at a *4X* value.
- Please remember that this is an arbitrary model that Professor Moyer may think fair, but you are welcome to come up with your own model. *The important thing is to agree on a model.*

Let's take a look at how the units might accumulate after 3 months for a hypothetical company.

ACTION	VALUE	Multiplier	Units	% Equity
Engineer 600 Work Hours @ $40/hour. Took no cash salary	24,000	2X	48,000	
Contributed 2 computers	1,000	1X	1,000	
Contributed $5,000 of capital	5,000	4X	20,000	
Total Units Earned			69,000	29%
Social Media Specialist 400 hours worked at $25/hour. Took cash for half the time and took payment for 200 hours in units	5,000	2X	10,000	
Total Units Earned			10,000	4%
Finance Specialist 500 hours worked @ $35/hour; took no cash	17,500	2X	35,000	
Contributed apartment for working	3,000	1X	3,000	
Contributed capital of $10,000	10,000	4X	40,000	
Total Units Earned			78,000	33%
Outside Investors Contributed $20,000 of capital	20,000	4X	80,000	
Total Units Earned			80,000	34%
TOTAL COMPANY UNITS			237,000	100%

The beauty of the model is two-fold. First, the pie is increasing as more and more value is being added to the company. Second, the pie is being sliced and shared based on everyone's contribution. This model easily handles people leaving and entering the business. If you leave, you retain your units although they will become a smaller and smaller portion of the total pie. Another 3 months from now, the total units may grow to 600,000 units as more people are added, more time is put in and / or more money is raised. But, importantly, everyone is getting his *right* share of the pie. Furthermore, this share of the equity will change based on their proportional contribution.

The key to making this work is agreeing on the hourly rates and the multipliers and doing this consistently and fairly. People in several countries, including in the United States, have adopted this model. Please read his book to get a full and richer explanation of this elegant concept.

Raising Outside Money

If and when you have to raise outside money, there are an ever-expanding array of resources. Let's look at some common ones.

Family and Friends: This is the one that most people turn to, to get off the ground. Family and friends can be very supportive. But if the venture turns sour, important relationships may be damaged. Tread with caution.

Crowdfunding: This may be the best place to start. Kickstarter is the most well known platform, but competitors such as Indiegogo and Circle Up also are used ubiquitously. People want to support such ventures for the thrill of helping launch something (the Pebble Watch, for example) and getting the product, or some other goodies, as a token of appreciation. But even more importantly, this is an excellent way to do a test market, to get a reaction from real customers. It almost seems like a no-brainer to me. However, choose a crowdfunding company that does not demand any equity but only charges 6% or so of the money raised.

Neighbors: A recent article in *The Wall Street Journal* had the following heading and copy which says it all: "Entrepreneurs Turn to a New Source of Funds: Their Neighbors…Forget Buy Local. A Growing Movement Is Urging People To Take Grass-Roots Support Further And Invest Local." At the very least, it makes sense to share with your neighbors what you are doing and offer them an opportunity to participate.

Incubators: These are springing up in many cities wherein you can get a place to work, have access to services and mentoring for a limited period of time, all for a certain piece of equity. The competition to get in is quite intense and they tend to be technology focused. The *Y Combinator* is the granddaddy of them all, while *1871* leads the pack in Chicago.

Angel Investors: These are people who have already "made it" and can provide funding and at times good advice and useful introductions. But they do expect to get equity and at times their participation may be less than "angelic."

SBA (Small Business Administration): This is a possibility under certain circumstances.

Venture Capital and Banks do not really lend to startups.

A note of caution is in order. Even though I lean towards bootstrapping, there are legitimate times when outside funding is appropriate from the outset. Many of the companies that have grown rapidly, such as Uber, could not have done so without such outside capital. Also, I have emphasized the need for integrity in everything you do. However, not everyone in the world will behave that way. It is entirely appropriate to look after your interests and have a lawyer and / or an accountant review key documents before you sign anything. A good operating philosophy can be President Ronald Reagan's dictum: *"Trust but verify."*

Assignment: What is your funding plan?

You know my opinion - bootstrap it yourself for as long as possible. But it is your decision. How will you fund your venture? Use this checklist to make your determination

- ☐ Bootstrap – using Professor Moyer's model:
    - ☐ Model (Rates, multipliers etc.) agreed upon?
    - ☐ Team members fully understand and accept the model?
    - ☐ Arbiter agreed upon?

- ☐ Raising Money from Family & Friends
    - ☐ Can they truly afford it?
    - ☐ Have you explained the risks in depth?
    - ☐ Any chance this might jeopardize their well being?

- ☐ Neighbors – same questions as above
    - ☐ Can they truly afford it?
    - ☐ Have you explained the risks in depth?
    - ☐ Any chance this might jeopardize their well being?

- ☐ Crowdfunding: Choose a crowdfunding company that does not demand any equity but only charges 6% or so of the money raised.
    - ☐ Kickstarter
    - ☐ Indiegogo
    - ☐ Circle Up
    - ☐ Other

- ☐ Incubators

- ☐ Angel Investors: These are people who have already "made it" and can provide funding and at times good advice and useful introductions. But they do expect to get equity and at times their participation may be less than "angelic."
    - ☐ Values aligned?
    - ☐ Roles understood?
    - ☐ Can they provide help beyond money?
    - ☐ Will they be easy to work with?
    - ☐ Will they help you get better?

Always remember: The best time to raise money is when you do not need it.

"Do what you love and the money will follow." - Marsha Sinetar

Additional Notes

Chapter 24

THE PITCH

"Unless commitment is made, there are only promises and hopes; but no plans." - Peter Drucker

"If you plan on being anything less than you are capable of being, you will probably be unhappy all the days of your life." - Abraham Maslow

"Here's to the crazy ones. The misfits. The rebels. The troublemakers. The round pegs in the square holes. The ones who see things differently." - Walter Isaacson, "Steve Jobs"

~~~~~~~~

Key Topics in this Chapter

- Why a business plan is necessary

- The 10-slide Pitch deck

- The 10-page Business Plan

- The 1-minute Elevator pitch

- Assignment: Get It Done

Why A Business Plan Is Necessary

Why do you need a business plan? Isn't it just more paper, numbers and slides? Haven't you done enough work? Why not just plunge ahead with the task at hand?

This is not an unreasonable reaction to have. After all it is much more fun charging the barricades and starting the revolution rather than spending time getting the gear ready. This is a long campaign my friends. Preparedness is your ally. Can you explain your business succinctly? Or do words, thoughts, phrases and images engulf you as you try and paint a picture for your audience?

Your vast treasure trove of data needs to be harnessed into something cogent, something easily understandable, something believable, something - that in hindsight - will appear obvious. Simplicity is the ultimate sophistication. "Duh" is the desired response. That is why we write a business plan, develop a slide deck and practice an elevator speech. To explain, to persuade and to gain commitment.

What should you work on first? Some people like developing their ideas with slides while others prefer the written word. Start with whichever one you feel more comfortable with.

The 10-slide Pitch Deck

By now, you must have memorized these 10 slides.

```
1. Problem / Solution
2. Product
3. Customer
4. Competition
5. Marketing & Sales
6. Business Model
7. Financial Plan
8. Funding
9. Team
10. Timeline
```

We will discuss the best way to make a compelling presentation in the next chapter. For now, let's look at how you might construct a powerful slide deck.

Tell a story. Human beings love stories, stories that involve them and make them feel an emotion. Use this slide deck to tell such a story.

Pictures tell the story better than words. Some slides will undoubtedly have numbers, charts and copy. Whenever possible use a picture. It is far more evocative. The picture will set the stage. You will provide the narrative.

The first minute is crucial. You will either engage your audience or lose them in those first 60 seconds. Make your starting slides really count.

Make the slides easy to read. Most presenters think of slides as an extension of their notes. Their copy is long and hard to read and impossible to follow. Clear, easy to read, enjoyable presentations are a rarity. Be the exception.

Use a minimum 28-font. You are undoubtedly thinking "This will limit me to putting only a few words on a slide." Exactly. That is the idea.

Why only 10 slides? Think of this as the initial deck. In most cases, you will be given 10 - 20 minutes for a presentation, which might include questions. Great story telling does not require a profusion of words. Spend more time on listening and answering questions.
"Brevity is the soul of wit." - Shakespeare

10-slide Questions deck. I have seen a fair number of presentations in my life and I am always struck by how infrequently a presenter has the appropriate slide to answer a question. Separately develop a slide for the 10 most asked questions. You will have the audience in your hand. It will show that you actually thought about what questions might arise. It will also show that you were prepared with a crisp and credible answer.

50-200 slide decks. The reality is that you will develop many more slides to share greater details for every facet of your business. These are more than likely to be used at follow up meetings when people want to dig into the business in greater depth.

Start with the 10-slide deck. That is the most important assignment for now.

The 10-page Business Plan Write Up

Why only 10 pages? It is long enough to provide a reasonably complete picture and short enough that people might actually read it. Getting it down to 10 pages will not be easy, but no one said that clarity and brevity were simple.

Just like the starting slide deck, this 10-pager is to be used as an introduction. More detail can always be provided when asked for. This 10-pager has two parts:

1) A 2-page executive summary and **2) An 8-page business plan.**

2-page Executive Summary. You must distill the essence of your business proposition into only two pages. Use the same flow as the slide deck. If you get invited to speak to someone, send them this summary in advance. It will show them that you are well prepared and it will also help them prepare, resulting in a better meeting.

8-page Business plan. The flow is the same as the slide deck and the executive summary. Once again, you must hook the reader up front. They won't get to the last page unless they are captivated by the first.

Who should write it? Preferably, the best writer on the team. Business plans written by a committee are a torture. Set aside the egos and hand it to the person best equipped to write it. By all means provide inputs and feedback, but let the paper have the feel of just one voice.

Make it easy to read and attractive to look at. This advice almost sounds silly, but you'd be surprised how often this is not the case. Ensure that the layout is attractive. Don't try and cram in too much. An 8-point font with ½ inch margins is not attractive. Use an 11 or 12-point font. Provide headings where appropriate. Be clear when you refer to an attachment or an exhibit.

Attachments. In my class, I allow 6 pages of attachments. These also should be attractively designed and should be included to elucidate a point that has been made in the main paper. They can be pictures, charts, financials, or the results of a survey. Be sure to make them easy to read. In fact, each of these pages should be able to stand on their own without any further explanation.

The 1-Minute Elevator Pitch

Have you ever been on a rapidly rising elevator and tried to make conversation? Not easy. Time is short, actually only 60 seconds. The other person is only partially interested. Besides, there is distracting noise. You really need to get this person's attention. More than that, you want them to invite you back for a fuller conversation. Welcome to the elevator pitch. With a bit of practice, you will look forward to riding elevators.

Getting Ready. The fact is that you know your business well. You have lived and breathed it for several months. Now develop your version of Einstein's $E=MC^2$.

Consider developing a poster or a cartoon. Capture your idea in a picture and then describe that picture. The idea for Southwest Airlines, the story goes, was drawn on a paper napkin in a restaurant by Herb Kelleher and his partner.

Main points. You can't use all the points of the 10 slides. So what should you focus on? Consider the following:
* Problem / Solution / Your Product (You must capture their imagination here).
* Size of the opportunity.
* Who else is doing this and why you will win.
* Who are you and what do you need (Raising $X, would like to meet you next Tuesday).

Develop a tagline that captures the benefits. All the taste, half the calories. Here is another one: Twice the return, half the investment. You have my permission to use this, assuming of course that you can deliver on it.

Practice, Practice, Practice. Enough said.

Assignment: Get It Done

Not much to say. Go do it. I know you can. This work will be done on other sheets of paper and Keynote or PowerPoint slides. Use this checklist to review and complete the work.

Your Idea

☐ Is it a HECK YES idea?

☐ If not, go back to the drawing board and do a re-start. Better now, than later.

Suggested Slides (but feel free to change these to suit your needs)

1. Problem/ Solution
2. Product
3. Customer
4. Competition
5. Marketing and Sales
6. Business Model
7. Financial Plan
8. Funding
9. The Team
10. Timeline

The 10-slide Pitch deck checklist

☐ Do they tell a story?

☐ Have you used plenty of pictures?

☐ Is the font large enough (minimum 28)?

☐ Is the text easy to read?

☐ Is the first minute compelling?

☐ Do you have back up slide for 10 anticipated key questions?

☐ Do you have 50 detailed slides as a backup?

Then create a 10-page Business Plan document using this Checklist

☐ 2-page Executive Summary?

    ☐ If people only read this, will they fully understand the business proposition?

☐ 10-pages of attachments providing detail?

Does the plan read well?

☐ Is it cohesive (as opposed to being written by a committee)?

☐ Is it compelling?

☐ Do the attachments add the required depth?

☐ Are they laid out attractively and easy to understand?

One Minute Elevator Pitch (less than 100 words)

Write it here:

Now evaluate:

☐ Is it Cohesive? Does it make Sense?

☐ Can you present it smoothly?

☐ Is it COMPELLNG?

☐ Do you know what you want from the listener?

☐ Did you ask them for what you wanted (such as a meeting OR MONEY)?

I hear the elevator doors opening. Ready?

"And, when you want something, all the universe conspires in helping you to achieve it."
- Paulo Coelho, The Alchemist

Chapter 25

PRESENTING

"90% of how well the talk will go is determined before the speaker steps on the platform" - Somers White

""They may forget what you said, but they will never forget how you made them feel." - Carl W. Buechner

"Had the lecturer added 30 hours of preparation to his presentation, his 30-minute appearance would probably have inspired some of the 300 of us who were listening, but instead we stopped listening after about 30 seconds...." - Erik Drakenberg

~~~~~~~~

Key Topics in this Chapter

- Presenting

- Assignment: Practice, Practice, Practice

Mark Twain said: *"There are only two types of speakers in the world. 1. The nervous and 2. Liars."* Do you get a bit nervous before you go on stage? I know I do even though I have led companies and made umpteen presentations over the years. Perhaps these words of wisdom will quell those butterflies: *"The best speakers know enough to be scared... the only difference between the pros and the novices is that the pros have trained the butterflies to fly in formation."* -Edward R. Murrow

You will have to stand before many kinds of audiences: teammates, people you are trying to hire, potential partners, suppliers, investors, family and friends. Each talk will have the same theme with a twist, connecting you specifically to the person that you are speaking to. The two most important things I can tell you are:

1. Don't sell, or say, anything you do not believe in. Stand for something.
2. Be genuine. Make every single person you meet feel important.

Presenting

My colleague and entrepreneur, Professor Michael Moyer[41], has written *Pitch Ninja* to help teams make dynamite presentations. He is always a favorite guest of my students, who end up making great presentations on the final day. I have developed the checklist below based on my own experiences, including what I have learned from Mike.

1. *Practice, Practice, Practice.* Everyone raves about the presentations that Steve Jobs used to make. Do you know how much he practiced? Days and days. Practice is the key. First practice alone. Then practice in front of something or somebody: the mirror, your cat, your friends and just about anyone who will listen to you. Over time, you will get good.

2. *Who should speak?* For classroom presentations, everyone on the team is encouraged to take part in the presentation. In the real world, it will generally be the CEO who will do all or most of the presenting. The team should be involved in answering the questions.

3. *Be fully vested.* From your body language to your tone, the audience will detect if you are passionate about what you are presenting or just going through the motions. If you are not vested, why should they be interested?

4. *Tell a story.* Don't repeat what is on the slide, but weave a tale. Take the audience on a journey. Emotion trumps facts any day. Remember you will hook, or lose them, in the first minute.

5. *Keep it simple.* Avoid big words, acronyms and jargon. They are a quick way to lose your audience.

6. *Know your audience.* Every audience is different. In a shark tank style contest on campus, there are the judges and then there is the audience. While you want to present to everyone, be mindful of the decision makers. In a meeting with a company, several people may attend, but understand where the decision-making power lies.

7. *Connecting with people.* Look people in the eye, gently. Connect with them. You will draw energy from that exchange and they will want to be involved in your story. People remember most how they felt, not how fancy or brilliant the presentation was.

8. *SMILE. ALWAYS SMILE.* There is a reason I wrote this in all caps. It is crucial. We buy from people we like. We like smiling people. We prefer to connect with those with an upbeat attitude. It cannot be a fake

---

[41] Moyer, Mike. *Pitch Ninja*. Lake Forest, IL: Lake Shark Ventures, 2014.

smile; it must come from within. You have worked hard to get in front of people. You have something to share with them. Be grateful for this opportunity. Show it in your smile. Professor Moyer suggests putting a rock in your shoe to give yourself a physical reminder to smile.

9. *Modulate your voice.* Some slides call for excitement, others raise a question and some provide only facts. Each of them has a tone associated with it. Adequate practice and learning to relax during your pitch will help you modulate your voice.

10. *Answering questions.* The first thing to do is to listen carefully. Do not interrupt the speaker. Do not, I repeat, do not try to upstage him. Paraphrase the question to ensure that you have really understood the question. That is both respectful and also gives you time to develop your response.

11. *Never argue.* Never. Listen respectfully. If you have a perspective, share it respectfully. "Let me think about it some more," is always a good answer.

12. *Handling plaudits and criticisms.* Listen and thank the speaker. Do not defend, elaborate and never, of course, argue.

13. *"I don't know the answer right now."* That is also a perfectly good response. Tell them that you will get back to them and then make sure you do. Always keep your commitment.

14. *Be sure to thank everyone sincerely before you exit the stage.*

15. *Logistics.* This may be the most important part of this checklist.
    - Get to the location early.
    - Make sure that you know what equipment you will be using, especially if you have to use the house equipment.
    - Be sure to have the right connectors.
    - If possible, do a dry run on the premises to make sure the equipment is working.
    - Be certain to have your laptop charged. I once had a team presenting a business plan on an IT consulting idea. No one on the team had a charged computer or an extension cord to plug into an outlet. That was one embarrassed and sorry team.
    - Do not do anything that involves a web connection. For some reason the web gods take particular delight in going on break when you need them most. Download what you need in advance.
    - Consider getting your own projector to ensure that you will be able to give your presentation in the way you want to. They have become quite inexpensive.
    - I prefer not to give the listeners a hard copy of my slides before I present, because it distracts them. I am happy to provide a copy of my slides *after* the presentation.

Nothing on this checklist is difficult or unreasonable. Taking care of the small details will allow you to give a superb presentation. The difference between being good and being excellent lies in the attention to detail. Finally, be yourself. Be authentic. And, as always, approach everything with integrity.

"The secret to selling great work is to sell the idea of the work before you sell the work." - Peter Coughter, The Art of the Pitch

Assignment: Practice, Practice, Practice

Tattoo this Checklist onto your mind:

☐   I / We have practiced Practice _____ times.

☐   We know our material cold.

☐   We will tell them Captivating Stories.

☐   We will bring the decision makers into the story.

☐   We will connect with the audience.

☐   We will Enjoy ourselves while presenting.

☐   We will Smile a lot.

☐   We will Thank the people often.

☐   We will Listen to the questions intently.

☐   We will answer them Respectfully.

☐   We will always exhibit the highest level of Integrity.

Are You Ready?

Then Break a Leg!

Metaphorically Speaking Only.

PART VI

THE PATH AHEAD

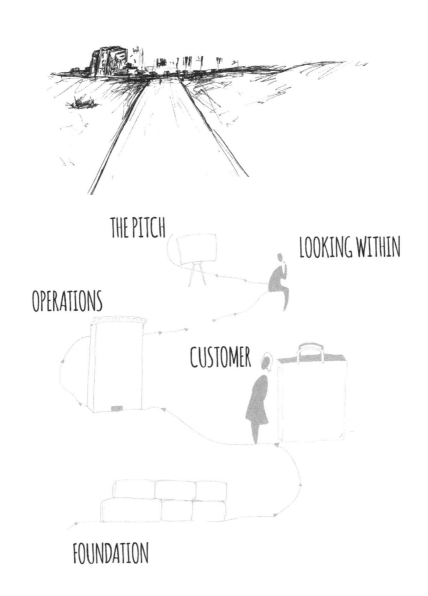

Chapter 26

THE PATH AHEAD

"If you have a dream, you can spend a lifetime studying, planning, and getting ready for it. What you should be doing is getting started." - Drew Houston

"Some beautiful paths can't be discovered without getting lost." - Erol Ozan

"We shall not cease from exploration, and the end of all our exploring will be to arrive where we started and know the place for the first time." - T. S. Eliot

You have come far. There is much more to learn about entrepreneurship in the years to come, but you have the basic building blocks to get started *now*.

It is time to discover the entrepreneur that is within you, put it to work, polish it and grow it. I hope you will create wonderful new businesses, assemble great teams that will mesh mellifluously, serve and wow your customers. You are likely to make more than a good living as you pursue your passion. I pray that you will live out all your dreams.

Let me bring this book to a close by offering you a few reminders for the road as you set off.

Entrepreneurship is a process. It is a discipline. Employ it. Persistently. Repeatedly. The results will come. The world is full of problems and shortcomings and therefore full of opportunities. Remember the entrepreneur's mantra: Problem - Solution.

You do not have to do it alone. Entrepreneurship need not be a solitary sport. Every idea requires a multiplicity of skills. It is unlikely that you alone will have all the necessary abilities. Assemble a great team to complete the jigsaw puzzle.

The right people make an endeavor exceptional. Hire people better than yourself. Create a culture of collaboration, growth, joy and service. Not only will you have a good time, but you will also achieve much more.

Get things done. Talk is cheap. Figure out what needs to be done, by when, by whom and then get it done. Delegating responsibility and holding people accountable is a necessary part of this DNA. Remain focused. Don't chase shiny new things. What you are doing will sometimes look boring and not as exciting as what's out there. This feeling is an illusion. Block out such thoughts and finish what you have started.

Develop a business model early on. Have a clear idea, or a hypothesis at the very least, as to whom you will sell to, at what price, what it will cost and what the profit will be. Making money is a necessary condition to be, and to remain, in business. Do not apologize or feel guilty for making money. Make lots of it, but always honestly.

No Customer, No Business. The only reason for a business to exist is to serve a customer. Do not take your customers for granted, do not mistreat them and do not ignore them. If anything, get to know and understand them better than they understand themselves. Make them come alive in your imagination and visualize your business putting a huge smile on their faces.

Be prepared for Plan B or even Plan C. Be ready for the whole length of the alphabet. A business, like life, rarely moves in a straight line. Be prepared to re-evaluate, pivot, change direction, refresh, renew and restart. Do not be discouraged. Embrace persistence and resilience.

Cash is the Oxygen of a business. Unlike in an airplane, no masks will drop to give you an extra whiff of oxygen during turbulence. Monitor cash carefully. Try and have a year's worth on hand. Be frugal with it and keep as many costs as variable as possible at the start.

Practice your pitch. And then practice it again. And then again. Maybe 50 times. Be ready for the short elevator ride that may change your life. Simplicity is the ultimate intelligence and the sublime sophistication. Make it easy for people to say "yes." Remember they are buying into your idea and also making a bet on you.

Embrace, relish and savor the journey. Life is not a destination. It is the journey. And the journey is the real reward. So make something of this adventure. Discover the infinite capacity that lies within. Make integrity your hallmark. Find a cause far greater than yourself. Serve. Give. And Live.

The path ahead beckons. God speed.

With respect and gratitude,

Verinder K. Syal

NOW GO

AND

CONDUCT *YOUR* SYMPHONY

EPILOGUE

"Did you use your 10-slide approach to make this book come to life?" I chuckled at the question, thought about it and answered "yes." Writing and publishing this book has all the hallmarks of a (not-for-profit) entrepreneurial expedition. Let's take a look.

1. *Problem / Solution:* I believe that the United States is suffering from a severe case of underemployment. Millennials have graduated in force, but are working as baristas and baby-sitters, frittering away their enormous talents. At the same time, change is occurring at warp speed opening up almost unlimited possibilities. Entrepreneurship provides a means of living. It also allows you to live life on your own terms.

2. *Product:* A simple, easy-to read, book that lays out – step by step – the time-tested pieces of the entrepreneurial jigsaw puzzle.

3. *Customer:* The Millennials are the beachhead target, although the principles transcend any age group. Everyone who dreams of being an entrepreneur, but is not sure how to get started, is my customer. This book is the way to attend my class.

4. *Competition:* There are hundreds of books written on this subject, including a few good ones. What, then, is my point of difference? I have tried to demystify the secret sauce of entrepreneurship and make it accessible to anyone who is willing to follow a process, be disciplined, work very hard, and live with integrity. These ideas are based on a lifetime of successful business experiences and several years of teaching award winning classes.

5. *Marketing and Sales:* This is a challenge. I am not a well known figure. Success will come through word of mouth, through referrals from people who find the book compelling and, while sales may build slowly, I anticipate the book to stand the test of time.

6. *Business Model:* "How will this book make money?" was not a question I focused on, since that was not my motive for writing the book. My goal was to share my knowledge and to help others achieve the American dream as I have. Therefore, I decided to make the book eminently affordable by pricing it like a best-seller rather than an expensive text book.

7. *Financial Plans:* I did not do any long term financial plans though they may become necessary as the book achieves success. To date, the expenses to complete the book amount to several thousand dollars. Editing, book covers, website redesign, getting the manuscript ready to publish on Amazon and the Kindle all require money.

8. *Funding:* This is a self-funded project. I worked on the book diligently for more than a year, but did so in my spare time, while continuing my regular consulting and teaching work unimpeded.

9. *The Team:* This was the key that made both the product better and the journey enjoyable. I assembled a small team of young people, across two countries and three cities, to help edit the book and develop the illustrations. Later on, I reached out to three beta readers and a professional editor for feedback. Several of my friends provided me detailed feedback, and proof reading, that was invaluable. While I wrote the book, the team made the work significantly better.

10. *Timeline:* I have often said that "getting things done is hard." The presence of a common goal, clear deadlines, responsibility and accountability allowed us to meet our deadlines. We used Asana.com to lay out the timetable. This consisted of my revising two chapters each week, which were then edited twice by the team and me, and then I would do a final review before we called it a wrap. Illustrations were added as they became available per the timetable. Later on, we tacked on dates for professional editing, beta reader feedbacks, comments and reviews from friends and readers, book cover and internal format designs, and uploading to Amazon. We also added a few weeks of contingency time. The book is being published on schedule. Whew!

What else do I want to share? Last year, a publishing company and I developed an idea for an online class for which we shot the introductory pilot. Unfortunately, they ran into financial difficulties and had to regretfully scrap the project. However, by then, I had gotten intrigued by the idea of sharing my knowledge with the widest audience possible. Later that summer, a several-week intensive class I had been planning to teach in Colorado got canceled at the last minute. I mused: Six free weeks, not one single appointment, the house all to myself in Colorado, what could I possibly do? The Gods smiled, the answer appeared, the book demanded to be written. I am somewhere on Plan D of this adventure today. I wonder what Plan G will look like?

Believe. Commit. Get It Done.
Breathe. Smile. Be Grateful. Give.

ABOUT THE AUTHOR

I am a teacher, consultant, businessman and an entrepreneur. I wrote this book to share my knowledge with everyone who yearns to become an entrepreneur. I have lived the American dream and I want to help you do the same.

I have led large businesses such as Quaker Oats Breakfast Foods, Rice-A-Roni, Ghirardelli Chocolate and Stella Foods. I have been an entrepreneur starting Filterfresh Coffee of Chicago with a partner, as well as my own consulting company. I have succeeded at many things and failed at a few. But for the most part, I have been very lucky to do the things that I had a passion for.

Did you enjoy the book? Did it help you? What worked for you? What could have been better? Please drop me an email and share your thought and ideas with me at verinder@thoughtfulsimplicity.com. I would also appreciate your writing a book review on Amazon.

Occasionally, I publish a newsletter. If you would like to be on that list, please also send me an email. Your address will never be shared, and you can unsubscribe at any time. Provide Link for Kindle.

Most importantly, I want to urge you to start your entrepreneurial journey *now*.

Be Well,

Verinder Syal
Thoughtful Simplicity, Inc.

BIBLIOGRAPHY

1. Wolf, Martin. *Why Globalization Works*. New Haven: Yale University Press, 2004.
2. Dickens, Charles. *A Tale of Two Cities*. London: Chapman & Hall, 1859.
3. Drucker, Peter. *Innovation and Entrepreneurship*. New York: HarperBusiness, 1985.
4. Bridge, Rachel. *My Big Idea*. Philadelphia: Kogan Page Limited, 2006.
5. Jordan, Robert. *How They Did It: Billion Dollar Insights from the Heart of America*. Northbrook, IL: Redflash Press, 2010.
6. Seelig, Tina. *What I wish I knew when I was 20*. New York: HarperCollins Publishers, 2010.
7. Godin, Seth. *Purple Cow*. New York: Penguin Group US, 2003.
8. Lencioni, Patrick. *Five Dysfunctions of a Team*. San Francisco: Jossey –Bass, 2002.
9. Shakespeare, William. *Othello*. UK: Thomas Walkley, 1622.
10. Wickman, Gino. *Traction*. Dallas: BenBella Books, Inc., 2011
11. Wickman, Gino. *Get a Grip*. Dallas: BenBella Books, 2012.
12. Mullins and Komisar. *Getting to Plan B – Breaking Through To A Better Business Model*. Boston: Harvard Business School Publishing, 2009
13. Source: eMarketer
14. This data is from Restaurant Association and is for Fiscal 2013.
15. Aulet, Bill. *Disciplined Entrepreneurship*. Hoboken, NJ: John Wiley & Sons, Inc., 2013
16. Kaputo, Catherine. *Breakthrough Branding*. Boston: Nicholas Brealey, 2012.
17. INSEAD: Michel et Augustin Cookies: Culinary Adventurers Competing Against Food Industry Giants
18. *Forbes*: May 2010: "Best-Loved Advertising Taglines"
19. Holmes, Chet. *Ultimate Sales Machine*. New York: Penguin Group, 2007.
20. Sewell, Carl. *Customers for Life*. New York: Doubleday Business, 1990.
21. Deaver Brown and Cross River Inc., HBR
22. Ziggy 2015, Yahoo cartoons
23. July 2010 Harvard Business Review
24. http://consumeronomics.anoj.net/2013/09/caffeinonomics-1-pricing-cup-of.html
25. Freiberg, Kevin & Jackie. *Nuts!* New York: Bard Press, 1996.
26. "What Makes a 5-Star Hotel? Top 10 Things to Look For" by Hilary Stockton
27. Case UVA-ENT-0027 by Professor Andrea Larson of the Darden School of Business Administration, 1997.
28. Burns, James MacGregor. *Leadership*. New York. HarperCollins, 1978.
29. Kotter, John. *A Force For Change*. New York: Free Press, 1990.
30. Collins, Jim. *Good to Great*. New York: HarperBusiness, 2001.
31. *How Good People Make Tough Choices"* by Rushworth Kidder. See Bibliography.
32. The US is ranked #19 out of 175 countries on the 2014 Perception Corruption Index done by Transparency International.
33. David Miller, PhD
34. "Law and Manner, " The Atlantic, 1927, by Lord John Fletcher Moulton
35. "Most Honest Cities: *Reader's digest* "Lost Wallet" Test, Reader's Digest 2015
36. Christensen, Clayton. *How will you measure your life?* New York: HarperBusiness, 2012.
37. George, Bill. *True North*. San Francisco: Jossey-Bass, 2007.
38. De Mello, Anthony. *Awareness*. New York. Random House, 2011
39. Csikszentmihalyi, Mihaly. *Flow*. New York: HarperCollins Publishers, 1990.
40. Moyer, Mike. *Slicing Pie*. Lake Forest, IL: Lake Shark Ventures, 2012.
41. Moyer, Mike. *Pitch Ninja*. Lake Forest, IL: Lake Shark Ventures, 2014.